Julianne Miles has supported thousands of people in their path back to work after a long career break, over the past two decades. A chartered psychologist and a successful returner herself, she is an internationally recognised expert on returning to work and a pioneer in the development of corporate returner programmes.

After running her own career psychology practice, Julianne co-founded Career Returners in 2014. Career Returners (careerreturners.com) is a social impact organisation that supports a global online returner community, partners with leading employers worldwide to create routes back to work, delivers return-to-work employability programmes and provides returner guidance for government bodies.

Julianne's mission is to make career breaks a valued part of a lifetime career. She was awarded an MBE in 2019 in recognition of her pivotal role in changing the landscape for UK returners. She lives in London, England and has two adult children.

Julianne Miles

Return Journey

How to get back to
work and thrive
after a career break

PIATKUS

PIATKUS

First published in Great Britain in 2025 by Piatkus

1 3 5 7 9 10 8 6 4 2

A CIP catalogue record for this book
is available from the British Library.

ISBN: 978-0-3499-44030-9

Typeset in Optima by M Rules
Printed and bound in Great Britain by Clays Ltd, Elcograf S.p.A.

Papers used by Piatkus are from well-managed forests
and other responsible sources.

MIX
Paper | Supporting
responsible forestry
FSC
www.fsc.org   FSC® C104740

Piatkus
An imprint of
Little, Brown Book Group
Carmelite House
50 Victoria Embankment
London EC4Y 0DZ

The authorised representative
in the EEA is
Hachette Ireland
8 Castlecourt Centre
Dublin 15, D15 XTP3, Ireland
(email: info@hbgi.ie)

An Hachette UK Company
www.hachette.co.uk

www.littlebrown.co.uk

Contents

Introduction

There is often a time in our lives when we want, or need, to press pause on our careers. You may have taken a career break to look after young children, to support teenagers through exams or mental health problems, to care for elderly parents or a partner with a terminal illness, to recover from cancer, burnout or bereavement, to relocate to a new country, or for a whole mix of reasons. Now, after two years, ten years or twenty years, you're ready to get back to fulfilling work. And, if you're thinking *That's easier said than done*, this book is for you!

You may have done no paid work at all for many years. You might have been working, here and there, on a small scale, or perhaps you have set up your own small side hustle or business. Now you're ready to ramp your career back up, but you're finding it daunting. Perhaps you've lost confidence and are questioning whether you're even employable. You might be stuck wondering what to do next or how to go about finding a job after many years out of the workplace. You might even be at the point of losing hope, because you've applied for hundreds of jobs and have got absolutely nowhere – and now you're thinking *Where do I go from here?*

How can I help? In this book I will draw on my decades of experience to consider the challenges you might face all the way along the return-to-work journey – psychological, practical, societal – and I will help you to navigate your way through, using a mixture of advice, coaching exercises and psychology research.

I'm a returner myself. More importantly, I am a leading return-to-work expert and a Chartered Psychologist. Over the years, I have supported many thousands of people in their return to work, initially through my own career psychology coaching practice and, since 2014, through Career Returners, a social business I co-founded to enable professionals who have taken long career breaks to return to work.

At Career Returners, we have partnered with over two hundred leading employers to bring over four thousand professionals back into skilled jobs, with the support of our Career Returners Coaching. We introduced the concept of returnships and other returner programmes into the UK and Ireland and now work globally. We have partnered with the UK and Scottish governments to run career coaching and job skills programmes for a variety of groups of returners, including parents and carers, and professionals in financial need. What's more, we provide advice, inspiration and connection to over ten thousand more returners worldwide through our Career Returners Community. I was proud to be awarded an MBE in the Queen's Birthday Honours in 2019 for Services to Business and Equality, in recognition of my role in changing the landscape for returners in the UK.

With all this experience, I can assure you that it is possible to get back to a great job, even after decades away. But I also know, very well, that it's not easy. You are not alone if you're finding it tough. Much of society and the employment market worldwide is still working from an outdated perception that successful careers are linear, without gaps. This leads to a frustratingly high level of recruitment bias against candidates without recent experience. That bias leads, in turn, to the 'career break penalty', whereby too many returners end up taking jobs well below their skill level, or not getting back at all.

It seems clear to me that career breaks should be viewed as a valued part of a lifetime career, with employers recognising the wealth of skills and perspective gained during and because of those breaks. This is my personal mission, which I've been championing since 2014 through Career Returners. I see this as the future of work. We're all living longer lives and we know that we will likely be working for forty, fifty or more years. Clearly, most of us are going to want or need to take a career break at some point.

The great news is that many employers around the world are waking up to the power of the returner. It's a good time to be returning to work! And, just as importantly, there are well-proven actions and mindsets that you can adopt to take yourself successfully along the road back to work. It doesn't matter how long your career break has been, what sector you're in, or where you are in the world – you can get back into fulfilling work that fits with your life, and this book will show you how.

How to use this book

The following pages provide a step-by-step route map for the road back to work: from starting out, to searching and applying for jobs, through to the first six months of transition into a new role. Getting back to work successfully has both a psychological and a practical side. First, you need to do the mental groundwork. You need to believe that it's possible to return, be clear on why you want to return, and get your mind and confidence in the right place. These are the foundation steps that will help you to keep moving forward, to maintain your motivation, resilience and determination along what is often a long and winding road.

The book is dotted through with returner case studies, to bring to life the challenges, the advice and the coaching exercises. I've created these case studies as anonymised composites, to maintain individual confidentiality, but they are all very much based on the thousands of real returners that I have met and supported on their path back to work, personally as a coach, and through my brilliant team of return-to-work coaches at Career Returners.

What can you expect from the book?

Part I covers Starting Out. It will help you to feel positive about your decision to go back to work, to understand your motivations, to boost your confidence, to reinforce your sense of possibility, and to decide which direction you'd like to head in.

Part II covers Finding Work That Works. It will show you how to identify more specific opportunities, how to craft and hone your 'career break story', and how to succeed at applying for jobs.

Part III covers Thriving Back at Work. It will provide you with tools and advice on getting ready to go back to work, adjusting to a new work–life balance, rediscovering your professional identity and coping with the emotional rollercoaster of the first six months back.

Some parts of the book will be chattier, more psychological, more macro – for example, the chapters on mental blocks (Chapter 1), confidence (Chapter 2), and the emotional rollercoaster of your early days back (Chapter 10). Some parts of the book will be heavier on practical detail, more like a workbook – for example, the chapters on setting your career compass (Chapter 4), how to talk about your career break (Chapter 6) and how to succeed in a return-to-work job search (Chapter 7).

I'll be sharing fundamental mindsets, tactics and creative ways of thinking to help you to tackle the challenges of getting back to work after a long break. You'll also find more detail on some of the psychology research and concepts underpinning my advice. This isn't a textbook, so inevitably there will be some simplification, but the references are at the back if you'd like to read more.

What I'm not going to cover are some of the more detailed job search logistics, or the ins and outs of setting up your own business. There are already myriad books and websites out there on how to write a great CV/résumé, build your interview skills and set up as an entrepreneur. As these practical aspects differ from year to year, country to country, and sector to sector, I'll leave it to you to look out for the relevant resources for your circumstances.

This book is likely to be most helpful if you work through it from the start, taking each set of topics and exercises in turn. But you can, of course, dip into specific chapters if you prefer, to solve a particular problem.

This book distils everything that I have learned in the last fifteen years about what works, and what doesn't, in the return-to-work journey. My hope is to provide as many career returners as possible with a clear, supportive and expert roadmap, to guide *you* back to fulfilling work that fits with your life, thriving and stronger than ever!

PART I

STARTING OUT

1

'Shall I, Shan't I, Shall I, Shan't I?'

How to Get Past Your Mental Return-to-Work Blocks

In 2001 I was on my own career break. I had previously worked in corporate strategy and marketing, in exciting international roles. When I had my daughter in late 1997, I didn't plan to take a long break. But life happened, we relocated from Australia back to London, all the interesting jobs at my level involved a huge amount of travel, good childcare was expensive and hard to find, and I felt a huge pull to stay at home to enjoy the early years. So I decided not to go back to work after my maternity leave. I then had another child and juggled baby and toddler with a house renovation. At this point, four years since my last job, I was starting to get itchy feet. But I was indecisive. Some days, all I wanted was to get back to my old job and not feel that my qualifications and experience were going to waste. On others, I wanted to do something completely different. And most days, I couldn't see past how complicated and stressful it would be to do anything at all beyond the caring responsibilities that subsumed my time and energy. I felt guilty about the potential impact on my family and unsure about how the logistics might pan out. These doubts kept me awake in the middle of many nights, inwardly debating the pros and cons – and that uncertainty held me up for fourteen frustrating months.

You may not have the financial luxury of choosing whether to go back to work or not. Or it might be that this really isn't the right moment for you to return: you might not be motivated enough yet, or perhaps your practical constraints are too demanding (we will come back to both motivation and practicalities later). Or you might have, like me, the urge to go back to something, but be procrastinating, flip-flopping and worrying.

'After a separation and imminent divorce, I'm now a single parent, and it is vital for me to become financially independent to support my family. But I relocated during my break and I am starting work in a new country, so the pressures are piling up. I feel so alone.' Bettina, marketing manager, after a six-year break

'I've had an awful three years after being diagnosed with breast cancer and coping with chemo, and now my confidence is shattered. I can't see the wood for the trees when I think about getting back to work. I can't even get over the initial hurdle of submitting a job application.' Chris, librarian, after a three-year break

'My main blocker in returning to work is finding a suitable job in my field that accommodates my family of three young children.

I'd love to find something that I could do during school hours or flexibly during holiday times, but this often seems impossible. My confidence and faith in my skills has also been significantly impacted by my career break and I sometimes feel paralysed by the two, which stops me from starting my search. I'm not even sure if I really want to go back.' Susanna, finance manager, after a seven-year break

Whatever the reasons for your ambivalence, anxiety or procrastination, this chapter can help. I'll shed light on some of the ways in which you might be stuck, and I will help you to gently loosen some of that stuckness. I cannot, sadly, remove all the practical barriers to returning (I'll tackle these in future chapters). But I can help you to cut through some of the mental noise, so that you can better understand your own thinking, feel more positive and get past your doubts and ambivalence. Overall, I can help you get out of the endless 'shall I, shan't I?' loop.

Here you are, like me, awake in the middle of the night. You're thinking: *I want a new challenge. Wouldn't it be great to be more intellectually stimulated, to go to meetings and contribute to meaningful discussions, to feel valued by colleagues?* You're thinking: *Wouldn't it be great just to put on work clothes and go to an office and have a chat over a hot coffee again?* But you're also thinking: *What if I can't do it? What if I fail? What if I've nothing to offer any more? What if everything's changed about work since I've been out? What if everything falls apart at home while I'm not there? What if I'm not physically (or mentally) up to going back? Is it too soon? Is it too late?*

Negativity bias: Velcro/Teflon

These kinds of fears and doubts are all too common. As neuropsychologist Dr Rick Hanson says, 'Your brain is like Velcro for negative experiences but Teflon for positive ones.' Your brain is hard-wired towards negativity: to let negative thoughts stick, and positive ones bounce away. This is coded at an evolutionary level. Because our brains evolved in the time of predatory sabre-toothed tigers, they're primed to scan for danger and shout about risk. It's better to be cautious than be eaten!

So your brain wants to keep you safe first, and fulfilment and happiness come way down the list. When you consider a major life change such as returning to work, your brain fires up its risk assessment: the negativity bias. And then, if you decide to stay put, your brain rewards you: a flood of reassuring chemicals in response to the promise of safety. But it's a short-term benefit, and you're still stuck.

Psychology: Negativity bias

Negativity bias means, essentially, that our brains respond more intensely to negative stimuli than to neutral or positive stimuli. Then, the negative weighs more potently in our decision-making than the positive. And, finally, negative emotions last longer than positive ones. It's a real triple whammy.

There have been lots of studies to identify and support negativity bias. Here are just a few examples:

- In 1998, Tiffany Ito and colleagues showed study participants thirty-three different photos, and measured their brain's electrical activity as they looked at them. They discovered that negative pictures (for example, a mutilated face) inspired more brain activity than neutral ones (like a plate) or positive ones (for example, people enjoying a rollercoaster).
- In a classic study by behavioural economists Daniel Kahneman and Amos Tversky, people who imagined losing $50 had a much stronger emotional response than those imagining winning $50. This is linked to a cognitive bias called 'loss aversion' (that is, the pain of losing is psychologically more powerful than the pleasure of winning).
- Psychologist Randy Larsen asked a diverse sample of people to keep detailed daily diaries, noting down their emotional experiences and how long those lasted. He found that negative emotions such as sadness, anger and anxiety lasted significantly longer than positive emotions such as happiness and joy.

We're smart people: rational, logical people. For most experiences, our brains are an asset, and we are used to them being on our side. It can therefore be tricky to recognise the moments in which our brain is working against us and to see our negative thoughts for what they are: a negative inner voice – beliefs *not* facts.

Sadly, our negative inner voice is very persistent. Trying to simply dismiss or ignore its negative messages doesn't often work.

When you try too hard not to think about a thing, it conversely takes up more space in your mind. As a mini-experiment to prove this to yourself, tell yourself not to think about something that's worrying you – you'll see that the more you tell yourself not to think about it, the larger it looms in your mind! However, you're not powerless, as there are various self-coaching techniques that you can use to help put your negative inner voice in its place:

- Give it a nickname, like your 'Gremlin' for example, then train yourself to spot and label the negative thought when it occurs: 'Here's my Gremlin again!' This helps to diffuse the power of the thought, separating you from the thought so that you can look at it more objectively.
- At the end of every day, reflect on, and list, three things that went well, and three things that you could improve next time.
- Try positive 'what-iffing' to reframe your thinking. By which I mean, turn all your negative 'What ifs' on their head:

  - Reframe 'What if I fail?' as 'What if I succeed?'
  - Reframe 'What if I hate it?' as 'What if I love it?'
  - Reframe 'What if I have nothing to offer?' as 'What if I have lots to offer?'
  - Stop for a moment and say to yourself: 'What if I *can* do this?' and see how good it feels to get a sense of hope and possibility.

- Test your negative thoughts using a coaching exercise called 'Balance the scales' (below).

Self-coaching exercise: Balance the scales

The aim of the exercise is to recognise your negative thoughts and balance them with more positive messages.

1   When the next negative thought about returning to work occurs to you, write it down. Quite often, the simple act of writing something down – drawing it out of your head and onto a piece of paper – diminishes its power.

2   Balance the thought. Use the more rational side of your brain to consider what evidence you have to support the thought, and then look for evidence to use against it. In other words, collect evidence to establish whether this thought is a fact or a belief.

3   Separate out your psychological barriers (those with limited or no factual base) from the practical ones. For now, just make a note of the latter, and put them aside. We'll look at how you can address practical barriers later on in the book.

4   Harness your inner champion. What would a good friend or supportive family member say to you in response to this thought you're having? Either ask them or imagine what they would say. Now write down these more hopeful messages. Next time the negative thought hits, re-read these messages, to turn up the volume on a more positive voice.

Negative thought	Evidence for	Evidence against	Psychological or practical?	Inner champion messages

Balancing the scales for myself

Back to my dilemma in 2002, after a lot of thinking and talking, I finally decided to go back to university to retrain as an occupational psychologist. I'd decided on my way forward, and I'd signed up for an intensive conversion course, with a lot of time in class and studying. I was excited by it, but I was still fretting in the night. These were some of the negative thoughts going around my head: my children have always had me around, they're too little, they won't cope without me; I'll be too tired and stressed, I can't do both things well enough. One morning, I did the 'Balance the scales' exercise for myself. I took a blank piece of paper, and I wrote my thoughts down. I considered what evidence I had to support my thoughts, looking for hard facts, not beliefs. I decided that it was true I would not be able to do school pick-up every day, but I could be around enough if I was back for bedtime. I knew from the developmental psychology books I had read that young children benefit in lots of ways from socialising at childcare. I called a good friend who went back to work a year before, and she told me that, although she spent less time with her family than she did before, she had more energy now in the time she does spend with them. Going back to work had made her happy and fulfilled, and she brought all that positivity back home with her. A few nights later when I woke up, worrying, I reminded myself of these positive things. And I went back to sleep.

Here are some other examples of balancing the scales, in action:

Balancing the scales – examples

Negative thought	Evidence for	Evidence against	Psychological or practical?	Inner champion messages
I can't do it. I'm too old and I've forgotten everything	I last interviewed for a job 15 years ago. When I did an online tech course, I found it so hard	I found a podcast with lots of people who went back to work at my age. I passed the course and can do more upskilling courses	Psychological	I have valuable skills that will come back quickly when I start to use them. I'm just out of practice!
No one will want to employ me after such a long break	I have sent out 50+ applications with no reply. A recruitment agency told me I need to start again	The podcast had people with even longer breaks. Some employers are running returner programmes	A mix of both	There are employers out there who will recognise my value
I'll never find a job that will fit around my family commitments	I can't do a long commute every day. There are few part-time jobs in my area	The world of work has changed. With hybrid working, I could probably make it work	A mix of both	Flexibility doesn't just mean part-time! Hybrid working could work for me
I don't have the energy to work	My days are really full. I'm very tired most of the time	Psychology research shows energy is not finite and can expand	Psychological	If I'm happier and more fulfilled, I will have more energy

There are a lot of themes we've pulled out here that we will come back to later in more detail: upskilling, job applications, the practicalities of arranging work around your life, and vice versa. For now, we are simply aiming to quieten your negativity bias and access a more positive voice.

Reinforce your positive messages

Pick out your best, most powerful inner champion messages, and then make them really visible. In the months when I was gearing up to return to study, I put a sticky note on my laptop that read: 'My family will be happier if I am happier and have more energy for them.'

These are some self-motivating messages that other returners have crafted:

- I have so much value to bring to an employer.
- I am talented.
- I am worthy and deserving.
- I have come so far – I can get there.
- What's the worst that can happen?
- I can do this – just take one step at a time.

Guilt

In describing my own experience here, and in my many years of working with returners, we uncover a very common negative thought: guilt. This might not be relevant in all cases (if you've had a health-related break, for example), but in my experience, guilt hits most strongly for returners with caring responsibilities:

particularly mothers, but also fathers, daughters, sons, wives, hus-
bands and partners.

I talk to Divya. She is in her late thirties and has two sons, aged
six and ten. She used to work in tech as a software developer
but paused her career to settle her family in after she moved to a
new country, and with one thing and another she didn't go back
to work. Her career break has now stretched to seven years and
she is starting to get the itch, the feeling that her brain has gone
idle. She enjoyed being a pioneering woman in tech and now
feels that she's wasting all those years of training. She still feels
ambitious – she wants to do more, but she tells me, 'I don't think
my boys can manage without me. They're so reliant on me. I feel
so selfish wanting to leave them.' Her mother and her friends from
the school gates are questioning her decision to go back to work.
She'd probably have to commute at least a few days a week, and
she's unlikely to even earn much after childcare and travel costs.
She's thinking: *Why can't I just be happy looking after my family?*

I'm not surprised that so many mothers decide not to go back
to work, even when they feel mentally unfulfilled at home. The
'selfishness' of working mothers is an idea embedded at a cultural, subconscious level. And the guilt message is pervasive:
in the media, in books and films, in the conversations I and my
coaches have had with hundreds of women. 'All working mothers
feel guilty, don't they?' is a phrase I've heard so many times, from
successful women in business as well as from returning mothers.
And it's a belief I always challenge.

Why does guilt exist?

Healthy guilt is a sign that our conscience is working effectively. It is there to tell us that we are hurting others, failing to do something right or actively doing something wrong.

Psychology: Guilt

Back in 1872, Charles Darwin proposed an evolutionary theory of emotions. He argued that emotions have a biological origin, which can be traced right back to our primitive behaviours. He suggested that different emotional states, such as happiness, sadness, fear, anger, surprise and disgust, developed to help us to respond effectively to our environment. Fear to keep us safe, disgust to keep us healthy, surprise to enhance our perception and response to stimuli, and so on.

The evolutionary benefits of guilt are not immediately obvious, so where does guilt fit in? The most influential explanation is Robert Frank's commitment model, which proposes a social – but still evolutionary – explanation. According to Frank, guilt provides built-in emotional restraint that reduces internal conflict within a group. It gives a group an evolutionary advantage by making members more reluctant to step out of line, and more likely to build bridges if they do cause harm to each other. This makes the group more harmonious and cooperative, increasing the likelihood of survival for everyone in the group. In this way, guilt became established as a core human emotion.

Healthy guilt, therefore, is a useful tool – a warning flag that leads (hopefully) to constructive change. But it is important, too, to take a step back. Guilt is an emotion that we experience because we believe we've caused harm to someone. The emotion of guilt follows directly on from thinking that you're responsible for hurting someone, whether or not this is the case.

So, feeling guilty doesn't *make* you guilty. Too often, guilt arises from judging ourselves by impossible standards, or being influenced by the perceived judgement of others. In these cases, it is not a healthy emotion but a destructive one, and it gets in the way of our quality of life. In caring for others, we get used to putting our needs at the bottom of the pile. And we decide that trying to make them more of a priority is selfish.

It's time to reframe that. We need to balance our needs alongside the needs of our families. How often, before having children or becoming a carer for a family member, did we label doing something positive for ourselves (playing a sport, learning a language, reading a book) as 'selfish'? Very rarely, I suspect.

Reassuringly, psychological research has found that work and family don't have to be in conflict: satisfying work can have a 'positive spillover' effect on family life. When we feel competent, satisfied and supported at work, we have more energy and a more positive outlook at home – and vice versa. Our different worlds actually 'enrich' each other. The truth of this is borne out by my own experience in years of working with returners. I've found, just as my sticky note reminded me, that returners tend to be surprised and relieved by the positive effects of combining work with family.

Psychology: Work–family enrichment

You probably have the feeling, some weeks if not most, that there just isn't enough time for all the things that need doing. If you add work back into the mix, you think you'll have much less time and energy. There won't be enough space for your partner, your children, your parents and your friends, or for exercise and general life admin. Is that right?

Traditionally, work–life balance researchers, such as Greenhaus and Beutell, would have agreed with this outlook, taking a zero-sum 'scarcity of resources' perspective: that each individual has a fixed pot of time and energy, and if they apportion any of that pot to a work role, they will therefore deplete the resources available for their family role. The end result is work–family conflict.

More recently, however, Greenhaus and Powell have proposed a more positive perspective to do with the 'expansion of resources'. They found that although work and family compete for our time resources, they can also be 'allies', with the balance of the two increasing our overall energy resources and improving our quality of life. Multiple studies have shown that thriving at work leads to gains in skills, social support and self-esteem, which improve the quality of family life and increase both job and family satisfaction (for example, S. Aryee and colleagues). And the transfer of positive experiences goes both ways: from family to work (feelings of support and achievement, and positive mood), as well as work to family (skills and confidence). Our two worlds 'enrich' each other. This is called 'work–family enrichment'.

Consider Maria, a mother of four who took on a new role as an administrator in a government education department after a ten-year break: 'Having a purpose makes me happier, more energetic and more fulfilled. I now enjoy being with my children more and look forward to the holidays with them rather than slightly dreading them.'

Or Giulia, who cares for her frail elderly mother and who recently returned to her previous employer (a large energy company) after a four-year break: 'I thought working was going to run me into the ground, but I now have more energy and patience with my mum than I had as a full-time carer. She seems to appreciate me more. Life is busy, but I feel back to being me.'

Identify your guilty feelings

The 'Red flag or red herring' exercise, below, can help you to identify your own 'guilty' feelings, and then to work out whether these are healthy or unconstructive.

Self-coaching exercise: Guilt – red flag or red herring?

Step 1: Self-reflection
When do your feelings of guilt come up?
What aspects of returning to work do they relate to?

Are these feelings justified? Do you really think you are making a decision that is inconsistent with your values? Do you really think that your home life will be poorer if you return to work? Is there evidence for your feelings that you are letting someone down?

Did you answer largely 'yes' to the questions above?	Did you answer largely 'no' to the questions above?
⬇	⬇
RED FLAG	**RED HERRING**
⬇	⬇
Step 2: Act to address the guilt	**Step 2: Act to address the guilt**
e.g. make a plan B	e.g. letting go
e.g. consider practical changes	e.g. constructing more positive messages

You can see how this exercise might look in practice, if we look at a couple of returner examples (see below). Once you've read these case studies, come back and write your own list of two to three 'address the guilt' actions here:

I helped Divya to analyse her feelings of guilt using the 'Red flag or red herring?' exercise. You can use our conversation as a blueprint for your own self-coaching. This, much like the last exercise, is to do with separating actual barriers from psychological barriers.

As a starting point, Divya told me that she felt selfish, because she's planning to leave her boys who are 'reliant' on her. On reflection, she explained that she wasn't worried about working within school hours. Her negative thoughts were most powerful at the start and end of the day – on the school run and at bedtime – when everything felt chaotic and her children didn't seem to be able to sort things out for themselves. When she imagined returning to work, she imagined herself being absent at these times of day, and she just couldn't see them getting to school on time, with everything they need, getting fed in the evening, and getting their homework done, without her. And she doesn't have grandparents nearby to help out.

On testing whether her feelings of guilt are justified, Divya tells me that the nature of her tech role means that she can work fairly flexibly. She says that it's important to her that she sees her children for some quality time every day, but that in fact the mornings are such a blur that she doesn't count this time as 'quality'. She acknowledges that her partner can get the boys ready and drop them off at school on some days, that they will need to become more independent and that, actually, this might be good for all of them. They could do an after-school club so, provided she could find a job where she gets home in time to pick them up, and perhaps work from home one or two days, it should be manageable.

Where we got to here is that Divya had no specific evidence for her statement that her family can't cope without her – just a general, underlying feeling that her work will negatively impact her family. She found the research evidence countering this belief to be reassuring.

Now to address the guilt. In Divya's case, as she's realised that her guilt is a red herring, she agreed to try to let go of the guilt, not to just accept it. She wrote down two positive effects to focus her mind on: (1) she'll be much more satisfied once she's back using her skills (2) her boys will have more time in the week to strengthen their relationship with their father.

When guilt is a red flag

It might sound as if I'm advocating that work is the right path for anyone on a caring-related break who isn't feeling fulfilled. But I meant it when I said at the start of this chapter that it may not be the right moment for you to return. I have worked with other people for who guilt *did* turn out to be a red flag.

For example Katia, who worked for years as a lawyer. She went back after maternity leave, so she's used to the juggle of being a working mother. She resigned to take a career break two years ago when her teenage daughter had serious problems with anxiety and depression. Then, last year, her eighty-five-year-old father was diagnosed with cancer, and she now goes to see him at least one day a week. She only ever planned to take a one-year sabbatical, and really misses 'the buzz' of her work. Her old boss called recently to ask if she's interested in coming back, and she feels a huge desire to say yes. But the job would involve long days and is very demanding. Her daughter is much better, but Katia still worries about her. She told me that when she thinks about returning to work she immediately feels 'awful' about the effect on her daughter and father.

I went through the same 'Red flag or red herring?' exercise with

Katia that I went through with Divya. And in the end Katia, unlike Divya, identified that there was a real incompatibility between her desire to return to the role she used to do and what she considered to be her essential responsibilities as a mother and daughter. This guilt was a red flag, not a red herring: the prospect of full-time work in her old role was at odds with the values she's laid out for her family life. This doesn't mean that she can't happily return to any form of work, but it does mean that she may need to explore a plan B that is more compatible with her life right now.

To cover step 2 – addressing the guilt – we talked about what practical changes Katia could consider, to bring her work and her values into line. For example, could she find a more flexible legal role with part-time hours? Could she think about a change of direction, using her transferable skills in an industry with more flexibility? Would she, ultimately, be better off waiting a while to go back to work, because this is a particularly demanding time at home?

A few months later, Katia tells me that she has decided not to return just yet. She realises that she has her heart set on returning to her old job at some point, but this isn't the right time. She wants to be fully present for her family for the next year, she will then think about it again. In the meantime, she's looking at doing some legal volunteer work for a charity.

All-or-nothing thinking and perfectionism

There is a concept in psychology called 'all-or-nothing' (or 'black-and-white') thinking, in which you see only the extremes, and no middle ground. The above discussions I had with Katia and Divya reveal the 'all or nothing' trap fairly clearly.

In the return-to-work context for a parent or carer this black-and-white thinking might look like:

Either I have a full-on, high-pressure, demanding job, like I had before, with no time and energy for anything else,

Or I don't work at all and stay home to look after my children/mother/father/partner.

When you imagine going back to work, you think: *if I can't commit to it totally, it's not worth doing. If I can't stay late, then I won't get all my work done, and I won't be a good employee. If I do stay late, I won't be a good parent/daughter/partner.* The thought of compromise becomes a roadblock that you can't get around, so you delay the decision. You wait until it's the 'right time', until life is calmer. But here is the difficult truth: as a parent or a carer, or as someone who has struggled with their own health, there will *never* be a perfect time to return to work. There will always be multiple demands on your time and energy.

What underpins this thinking is perfectionism: you set impossible standards for yourself. You want to be a perfect employee and also perfect in your personal life. You make this all worse with a reluctance to delegate (a classic perfectionist trait), because 'no one can do things as well as you can'. And still you continually feel inadequate.

There is a pervasive idea that perfectionism is not a real weakness, but is a positive indication of high standards, making us perform better. Psychology professor Thomas Curran says, in *The Perfection Trap*, that 'perfectionism is our favourite flaw'. Although some level of striving is a good, productive thing, it's important to know that the idea that 'perfectionism = achievement' is overall a myth and can harm our mental health (see psychology box below).

Psychology: Perfectionism

There is strong evidence that perfectionism results in worse rather than better outcomes. A 2018 review of multiple studies in this area by Harari and colleagues found that overall perfectionism is 'net detrimental'. In one study, by sports psychologist Andy Hill, cyclists were asked a series of questions to establish whether they self-identify as a perfectionist or not. They were then set a comfortably achievable time goal to race against. When told they had failed to meet the time, and to try again, the self-oriented perfectionists scored much lower on the second race than the non-perfectionists. Hill's conclusion was that their perfectionism led to feelings of shame, which caused them to give up.

Did you know that there are different kinds of perfectionism? Hewitt and Flett, leading psychologists in the perfectionism field, identified three clear facets: self-oriented perfectionism, other-oriented perfectionism and socially prescribed perfectionism. In other words, perfectionism might involve:

1 Setting very high standards for yourself.
2 Setting very high standards for other people.
3 Feeling the pressure to achieve high standards to meet the high expectations of others.

According to a meta-analysis by psychology professor Thomas Curran, it is the last of these – the societal pressure to be perfect – that is rising most rapidly in the USA, Canada and the UK, in line with an increased emphasis on 'competitive individualism'. He also reported that this is the type that is linked most strongly to mental health issues.

The upshot? Embracing the idea of being 'good enough' is more likely to lead to better outcomes, and better mental health, than trying to be perfect!

Back to Divya. When I first met her, she said to me, 'I can't see how I can go back to work and be happy with being "good enough" as a mother and at work. I want to get a more intellectual challenge, but I find it hard to compromise. I'm a perfectionist. Compromise feels like failure to me.'

I encouraged Divya to reframe compromise as a positive thing. Because if you have a full, rich, life, there will inevitably have to be trade-offs between your various priorities. As business professor Rosabeth Moss Kanter says: 'You can have it all. It just won't all be perfect.' She wisely suggests that we reject the perfection myth, choose our areas of excellence, ignore or 'let slip' others, and avoid turning trade-offs into 'insurmountable obstacles'.

For Divya, the question of 'shall I, shan't I?' return to work had a different answer depending on whether she approached the issue in an all-or-nothing way or with an attitude of compromise. If she asked herself, 'Shall I take a full-on tech job, like I had before, alongside all my family commitments?', the answer for her was no. But when she tried out asking herself, 'Shall I look for a fulfilling job in tech that fits with my family life?', she then felt much more positive.

In our work together on addressing her feelings of guilt, we'd touched on some of the compromises she was prepared to make with her family commitments. To help her to start deciding where

31

she can and can't compromise in a job, we looked at clarifying her motivations for wanting to work, using the 'Finding my why' coaching exercise below.

Divya's three key drivers are (1) intellectual stimulation (2) the social side (3) regaining her professional identity. We agreed that these are key aspects on which she shouldn't compromise, otherwise work is unlikely to be energising for her. When she envisaged herself back in a tech role, working in a team and using her brain again in a role in which she can still spend enough time with her sons, she felt her motivation building to move forward.

Self-coaching exercise: Finding my why (motivations)

Read through this list of common motivations for returning to work and write down the three that are most important to you (you can add any other factors that aren't listed). Then add a few lines on what each of these factors means for you:

1 Financial need
2 Having my own money
3 Intellectual stimulation
4 Social side/teamworking
5 Being a role model to my children
6 Being on a more equal footing with my partner
7 Having a sense of achievement
8 Regaining my professional identity
9 Having status
10 Tapping into unfulfilled ambitions
11 Avoiding fear of an empty nest

Finding my why

Motivation 1
What it means to me:

Motivation 2
What it means to me:

Motivation 3
What it means to me:

Your future self

If your mind is still going backwards and forwards, with an equally weighted list of pros and cons, it can be helpful to put aside excess rationality for a moment, and instead tap into your intuition. I encourage you to do this with a couple of imaginative 'Future self' exercises, designed to help you to inhabit a different perspective from your current point of view.

Self-coaching exercise: Advice from my future self

Exercise 1: Myself in Two Years

Imagine two different versions of your life two years from now and consider how you feel in each version.

Future version 1 Everything has stayed the same as it is now

How do you feel?

What are the positives?

What is missing?

Future version 2 You have returned to work

How do you feel?

What are the positives?

What is missing?

Which of these versions of the future feels more appealing and why?
Focus on how you're feeling rather than what you're thinking.

Exercise 2: Myself at Seventy

Imagine you are seventy, looking back at yourself today. What advice would you give?

Is your seventy-year-old self sympathetic to, or impatient with, your current indecision? What are they saying to you?

What advice would this future self give you: to return to work now, to wait a while longer, or to consider making a different change?

One final thought: change is hard

William Bridges, who has been researching life transitions since the 1970s, tells us that few changes are universally positive – even those that you've been wanting to make for a long time, such as moving house or getting a promotion. His transition model explains the three broad transition stages that a person experiences, as we psychologically come to terms with the new situation caused by a change: an Ending, the Neutral Zone and a New Beginning.

In my own experience, and from observing and talking to thousands of returners, these three stages ring true:

- Change often starts with more than a hint of sadness – as you leave something behind and recognise what you're losing.
- There is then an unsettling in-between period in which you have to let go of the old reality, but don't yet fully inhabit your new identity. You are in a psychologically uncomfortable limbo land and can have a huge urge to leap back to your previous comfort zone. But it's an essential time to re-orientate, as you mentally explore and adjust to the change.
- There is, finally, the positivity of feeling that you've entered into something new. You have fully taken on your new identity and feel a burst of energy, excited by your new direction. You've made it to the other side of the transition!

Perhaps you've written, and re-written, your pros and cons list for returning to work. You've been writing it for months. You're sure now that the pros outweigh the cons, but you're still finding it hard to move forward. It can help to acknowledge the aspects of your career break life that you'll miss, no matter how much you want to get back to your career. You can feel a sadness about what you'll be leaving behind: perhaps the control over your own day or the ability to spend so much time with your family. Feeling this sense of loss is a natural by-product of change – it doesn't mean that returning to work is the wrong choice for you. It may be that you just need to ride out the discomfort, to get through the tricky in-between period before you can wholeheartedly welcome your next chapter.

You may come to the end of all this analysis and find that the cons outweigh the pros. You cannot see your way back into the office, or how to add work into the balance of your life. Returning at all, or at least now, is not the right decision for you. What's important is that you have reached a positive decision about this – not guided by fear and indecision, or held up by procrastination, but informed by a proper assessment of what's important to you right now. Aim to put thoughts of work aside for a while – escape that shall I, shan't I indecision loop – and focus on other things.

If that sounds like you, there is one piece of advice from successful returners that I'd like to share here: keep your hand in, to keep your options open for the future. Consider engaging in some form of skilled work or knowledge building, no matter how small in scale (skilled volunteering, project work for friends and family, an evening class or a short course to update your knowledge of an existing field, or to try out a new field). This will keep up your confidence and your sense of your professional self, ready for another day when you might make a different decision about going back to work.

If you feel that you've moved forward – the balance of your lists looks right, and you feel energised – let's then move on to boosting your confidence (Chapter 2), seeing what's possible (Chapter 3) and deciding what to do next (Chapter 4).

Summary

- It's normal to have negative thoughts when you're thinking about going back to work after a long break. Separate what is fact from what is belief, to see if your hesitation is more psychological than practical. Change your mental soundtrack: quieten your negative inner voice with some positive messages from your inner champion.
- Guilt is a huge issue for returners, and for returning parents and carers especially. Engage your rational brain to work out whether your guilt is a red flag or a red herring. If it's a red herring, take action to reduce its hold on you. If it's a red flag, consider a plan B.
- Don't be held back by perfectionism or 'all-or-nothing' thinking. Instead, embrace compromise and remember that being 'good enough' at various things points to a rich, full life.
- Get clear on your main motivations for going back to work, as these are the areas where you don't want to compromise.
- Tap into your more intuitive side, by imagining how your future self would feel about the decision.
- Change is hard. Accept that there will be a sense of loss about what you're leaving behind, and get ready for an uncomfortable transition period.
- If it's not the right time to return, keep your hand in to maintain options for the future.

'Get really clear on why you want to get back to work and keep reminding yourself of this when you're struggling with the rights and wrongs of the decision. There's never a perfect time to return, but there is a time when you just have to take the leap.' Divya, now back at work as a software engineer after a seven-year break

2

'Who would want to hire me now?'

How to Boost Your Confidence

R ita was always a high achiever. She went to university a year
early, graduated with a business and management degree,
then moved back to her home town to take up her first job as a
trainee business consultant. Over the next fifteen years she worked
her way up through various roles and certifications, ending up as
an operations manager with a multinational organisation. Then,
out of nowhere, her mother had a debilitating stroke. The family
did their best for a while – muddling along between them with
a rota of daily visits – but before long it became clear that she
needed full-time support. Rita took a career break to look after her
mother: five years of caring, then some extra recovery time after
her mother died. Six months ago, Rita decided that she would like
to go back to work. She charted a relatively simple course through

the 'shall I, shan't I' dilemmas described in the last chapter. She's had a long, often hard, break, and misses her professional life. She is totally sure that she wants to be back at work. But she is finding it hard to move forward.

Rita's problem is that, despite all her experience and the things she achieved in her past career, she cannot find the confidence to take the first step. She tells me that her brain feels muddy from years of caring: from late nights and grief, and the smallness of the routines of illness. She has the sense that she has 'forgotten the basics'. Not just the crucial, technical components of her previous skillset but, more broadly, 'how to behave in the working world'.

She feels that even if she could overcome these things, the gap in her CV is 'too yawningly big' for anyone to take her seriously, and she's 'embarrassed' to send it out. She cannot see why some-one would employ her when there are all these smart, motivated, highly qualified young people around. She feels out-of-date, left behind, too old. 'Who would want to hire me now?' she says.

Rita's story is happening everywhere, all the time. The detail, of course, is different: a different kind of career, different reasons for a break, a different length of break. But a long career break typically wreaks havoc on the confidence of even the most capa-ble, qualified people.

'Who's going to want to choose a woman in her fifties over a fresh graduate?' Serena, media planner, after a twelve-year break

'I'm not sure I'm even employable', Jess, scientific researcher, after an eight-year break

'I'll never get my brain around the new technology', Joy, insur-ance analyst, after a five-year break

'What can I bring to a team after a decade out?', Tom, retail manager, after a ten-year break

'My confidence is on the floor', Erin, arts administrator, after a three-year break

This 'no one will want me', or 'I can't do it', feeling is pervasive, and can be paralysing. It can, for many people, throw up a barrier to returning to work that seems impossible to get over. It's certainly a hard one to tackle – that's why it has its own chapter! Just giving yourself a pep talk to 'be more confident' and repeating positive mantras is not likely to have much impact. But it is possible to slowly and steadily work your way back to confidence.

If you can't think yourself into confidence, what can you do about it?

What is confidence?

Let's first take a look at what confidence is, and what it isn't.

Confidence is a belief Confidence is your *belief* in your ability to succeed, not your *actual* ability to succeed. Ian Robertson, professor of psychology at Trinity College Dublin, talks about confidence as a 'bridge to the future'. You're combining 'can do' (a belief in your own abilities) with 'can happen' (a belief that your abilities will lead to the desired outcome). You need both parts for your confidence to shine.

Confidence is situation-specific, not general A lot of people are confident in one setting, but not in another. For example: you may be perfectly self-assured at home, among your friends, in wider social situations, but baulk at the idea of a networking event. It is helpful to separate work-related confidence (which is hit so hard by career breaks) from confidence in other contexts.

Confidence isn't a personality trait Confidence isn't a fixed quality, something that you're born with or without. It is absolutely possible to build and develop confidence.

Confidence isn't static Confidence ebbs and flows through your life, and even from moment to moment. You cannot, unfortunately, simply tick it off your to-do list. It's boosted when you're in your comfort zone, when you receive praise or recognition, when you can keep your achievements in mind. It plummets when you're in an unfamiliar situation, when you're criticised, rejected or ignored.

Confidence comes from action Taking action to move towards your goals builds your confidence. Confidence comes after action – it comes from doing, not thinking. Even getting ready to take action builds your confidence (see psychology box below).

Psychology: Deliberative vs implemental mindset

Studies by psychologists Hügelschäfer and Achtziger have shown that the positive effect of action on confidence is so powerful that it kicks in even when you're just planning to take action – before you even take the action itself.

Hügelschäfer and Achtziger took a group of students

---

and asked half to approach a question they were considering in their personal lives with a deliberative mindset. The students had to think: *Should I do X or not?*, and list the pros and cons of the action and non-action. Examples could be questions like, 'Should I move to another city after graduation or not?' or 'Should I buy a new car or not?' The second half of the group were encouraged to approach a similar question – a goal they wanted to achieve – with an implemental mindset. They started with the certainty of the action ('I will move to another city after graduation'/'I will buy a new car') and then they considered how they would go about it, listing the most important steps and pinpointing when, where and how they would carry out each step.

In essence: group one was encouraged to deliberate extensively, and group two was prompted to engage heavily with the actual detail of planning. The researchers then assessed confidence levels for each group. Across the entire group, confidence levels were higher within the implemental mindset than the deliberative. There were also gendered variations. Female students moved from under-confident to realistic, and male students from confident to over-confident (!).

The key takeaway: sometimes just moving up a gear – moving from more abstract thinking to actual planning – is the best thing you can do for your confidence.

Your professional identity

Let's go back to the concept that confidence is situation specific. Many people on a career break think nothing of taking the lead in their local community, or vocally advocating for their parent in healthcare settings, or settling into a role as the lynchpin of their social group. But they find themselves overwhelmed by self-doubt when they think about getting back to work.

What's going on here? It helps to understand that your work-related confidence – the belief in your ability to succeed in a professional setting – is tied very closely to your professional identity.

For most people, that identity (a version of themselves that dressed a certain way, commuted, had expertise at their fingertips, was relied upon by colleagues) fades or completely disappears during a career break. This erosion of identity happens, in general, so gradually that you don't notice it slipping away. Your answer to the question, 'What do you do?' is revealing in this respect. In the early days of your career break, you may have responded to the question with your profession or last job role, and the reasons why you're taking a break. Over time, as you start to feel less and less connected to the working world, perhaps you stop mentioning what you did before and talk purely about what you're doing now. Your 'work self' comes to feel, a number of years in, more like a distant memory than a core part of yourself.

This letting go of your old job title, and the credibility you feel it gave you, saps your confidence. This effect is magnified if you've taken on a caring role, which is so often undervalued by society, during your break. If you've ever replied to the question 'What do you do?' with 'I'm just a mum/dad', this point applies to you.

I've spoken to many returners who say that they feel they are a 'completely different person' after their break. Some shifts in your personality, experience and outlook are to some extent inevitable after a career break – even more so if you've gone through a major life change (a birth, a death, a relocation), as so many returners have. And there can be many positives within this shift: clearer priorities, a broader perspective, a refocusing of values, new experiences, skills and interests. But thinking of yourself as 'completely' different is unhelpful. It creates a chasm between the professional person you 'used to be' and who you feel you are now, dislocating you even further from your professional identity.

In the rest of this chapter we will take 'What is confidence?' into account as we think through some practical steps to help bolster your confidence in relation to work. I will support you as you:

- **Look back** To reconnect with the working person you used to be, and the professional skills and achievements you already have under your belt.
- **Think about yourself in the present** Who you are now, what your skills, values, priorities and strengths are, and what you've gained during your career break.
- **Connect with what might be possible in the future** To think about what you could learn and achieve from now on.

Looking back – reconnecting with your 'lost' professional identity

The first step in building professional confidence is to reconnect with the working person you were before your break. It doesn't matter if it was twenty months or twenty years ago. It doesn't matter if you feel like you are a completely different person now, or if your perspective, values and priorities have shifted more subtly in the years you've been away from your career. The things you accomplished during your career – the qualifications and experiences you gained, and the strengths and skills you built up – have not disappeared. You are still the same person who gained a professional qualification, built strong client relationships, managed a team, delivered complex projects or won sales pitches. These experiences remain a part of you, and those abilities are still there under the surface, no matter if you haven't used them (in a work capacity) in a long while. Even if your previous professional identity didn't feel authentic, and now you want to change direction, you will have many skills and experiences that you can take forward into a better-fit new role.

It's best to start with something really tangible, so focus on your specific achievements to date. Bringing these to the front of your mind can give your confidence a real boost.

Let's kick off this reconnection with a coaching exercise.

Self-coaching exercise: My life chapter achievements

1   Divide your adult life into chunks of two to three years each.

2   Give each chunk a label and a title, like a book chapter. This might be what you were doing at the time (university, first job, travelling, caring for children) and/or where you were located. Or use a more creative title – whatever works for you.

3   For each chunk, write down one to three things you achieved during that time. These achievements can be big or small and can be related to work, home or any aspect of your life.

Life chapter title	Achievement 1	Achievement 2	Achievement 3

Rita struggled at first with the 'My life chapter achievements' exercise. At the forefront of her mind were the caring years, which felt 'too formless and mundane' to pick out anything she'd call an achievement. But breaking the twenty-two years of her adult life into chunks definitely helped – as she set out the chunks, her achievements started to mount up. They ranged from getting her degree, to managing a team of twenty and winning an Employer of the Month Award in the process, to becoming involved with a running club and creating a friendship group when she moved to a new city. By the time she'd listed these and come back to her career break 'chunk', she was able to see achievement in how she had successfully advocated for her mother with medical staff: researching, coming to each appointment with clear notes and questions, and staying calm in a stressful situation: 'Before, the outcome was everything, and I was impatient get there as quickly as possible. I became so much more effective in communicating and I do think I got better treatment for my mother as a result.' Rita had 'forgotten' about most of her work achievements, but she didn't have to dive too far into her memory to pull them out again. By the end of the exercise she was starting to feel better.

Think about yourself in the present – recognise your core strengths

We move on from achievements to one of my favourite psychology concepts: the notion of core strengths. In everyday conversation we tend to use the language of 'strengths' and 'skills' interchangeably. But in psychology, strengths are subtly different from skills. Strengths are not abilities you have to work extremely hard at, or things that you are good at but that leave you feeling drained. You may count these things as skills, but they are not your strengths. By strengths we mean your innate talents: the things that you're naturally good at, that come easily to you, and that you are energised when using.

Psychology: Playing to your strengths

'Play to your strengths' is widely offered advice. But is there any scientific basis to it, or should we instead focus on improving our weaknesses? The field of positive psychology has investigated this question since 2000, pioneered by US psychologist Martin Seligman and championed by Gallup in the US and the Centre of Applied Positive Psychology in the UK. There is now a wealth of evidence that using our strengths really can get us a lot further, including these examples:

- Two different studies of university students, by Govindji and Linley and Proctor and colleagues, found that students who recognised and used their strengths more than their peers reported higher self-efficacy, self-esteem and wellbeing.
- Gallup surveyed over ten million people worldwide, over a decade, and found that people who have the opportunity to focus on their strengths every day are six times more likely to be engaged in their jobs and more than three times as likely to report having an excellent quality of life in general, than people who don't get to focus on their strengths (Roth, 2007).

49

- In a study of a regional community, Wood and colleagues found that people who reported greater use of their strengths over a six-month period increased their self-esteem and vitality and reduced their stress levels.
- In another student study, Linley and colleagues reported that people who used their strengths were more likely to succeed in achieving their goals.
- Employees who stated that they 'have the opportunity to do what they do best every day' were found by Harter and colleagues to be more engaged and have higher performance than other employees.

Knowing and using your core strengths is one of the foundations of rebuilding your confidence, as well as creating a fulfilling career. After a career break – however much you feel you've changed, or however out of date you feel your skills are – it is your strengths that will link the old you with the new you with the future you. And it is your strengths that differentiate you from the next candidate or a fresh graduate, even if their technical skills are more up to date. Your strengths are your Unique Selling Point (USP): the core of what you have to offer an employer.

Over the years I've asked many people to tell me their top three strengths. This question typically prompts a look of embarrassment, a long pause and then a struggle to get beyond one or two, often prefaced by, 'Well, I suppose I'm quite good at . . .' Most of us are far happier to reel off a long list of our weaknesses than to describe a few strengths.

Why is this so difficult? First of all, we tend to undervalue talents that come naturally and easily to us. We assume that because we don't find this particular thing hard, that means 'everyone can do it'. Added to this, many of us grow up with the message not to 'blow our own trumpet'. We're encouraged by societal norms to be modest or self-deprecating. This is all compounded by the fact that we often compare ourselves in each ability area with someone who is stand-out amazing, and so we decide we're not great at anything.

To help you to knock through all this self-deprecation, work through the coaching exercise on identifying your unique strengths combination.

Self-coaching exercise: Finding my USC (unique strengths combination)

The aim of this four-step exercise is to help you to identify your top three strengths. I call this your USC: unique strengths combination. This fits neatly with thinking of it as a type of USP in terms of what you have to offer an employer.

Step 1 Look back at your life chapter achievements (on page 47). Pick the four that felt the most satisfying: where you felt the most energised, most like yourself, at your best. Think about what strengths you were demonstrating in the execution of those achievements. What made you so good at what you were doing? Your strengths can be attitude-based (flexibility, positivity, calm under pressure), people-based (developing others, connecting others, managing others), task-based (goal setting and planning, decision-making, managing complex projects) or ideas-based (generating innovative ideas, strategic thinking).

My most satisfying achievements	My strengths demonstrated
1	
2	
3	
4	

Step 2 Ask your friends and family what they think you're particularly good at. Ask them to give you some concrete examples of you demonstrating that strength. Other people often notice your talents when you don't, plus you get the confidence-boosting benefit of some positive feedback. But do remember that you may have other strengths that they haven't noticed, that you show more in a work context. Note down the main strengths they mention.

Family and friends' feedback on my strengths

Strength 1:

Examples:

Strength 2:

Examples:

Strength 3:

Examples:

Step 3 Pick out two or three underlying themes which create a consistent link through your life (what we call a 'red thread' in coaching). Is there a role that you're always happy to take on? Do you love organising, and you're always the planner? Are you the innovative one who comes up with new ideas? Or the networker who thrives on connecting other people?

My red-thread themes

1

2

3

Step 4 Use all this information to identify your top three strengths (your USC), making them clear and specific, with credible examples to back them up.

A few things to remember:

1   Compare yourself to the average person, not the best in the business.

2   Think about what really differentiates you from the next person, rather than things that could describe anyone (like 'I work hard' and 'I get things done').

3   Create a specific distinctive phrase for each strength, rather than a one-word descriptor.

For example, if you were to drill down into what 'I'm good with people' means for you:

- 'I am good at pulling together and motivating a team of diverse people to work collaboratively to achieve a goal – like the leader of an orchestra.'
- 'I am good at making a connection with people of all backgrounds and building strong relationships.'
- 'I am good at coaching and developing others to achieve their potential.'

As another example, if you were to consider what 'I'm very organised' looks like in practice for you:

- 'I am good at project planning, co-ordinating other people, with a high attention to detail.'
- 'I am well-structured and good at organising my own time to manage multiple projects and deadlines.'

My USC

Strength 1:

Examples:

Strength 2:

Examples:

Strength 3:

Examples:

Write these strengths down and keep them in view (as well as in mind) as you carry on with your return-to-work process.

Rita recognises that she has always been good at communicating with people. Working off her list of past and career break achievements, she creates a specific phrase: 'I instinctively adapt my style of communication to work with each person – I love discovering areas of mutual interest and connection.' She also spots another general theme (a red thread) over the years in her ability to stay calm under pressure: 'When a situation becomes challenging and others get stressed, I become steely calm and can navigate a way through for myself and others.' Her friends help her to pinpoint her third strength: they point out that she has always been exceptional at project planning and delivery. A few examples they provide are, years ago, when she organised a reunion for school friends scattered across the country, and, more recently, when she put together a mind-boggling backup support rota for her mother.

By the end of the exercise, Rita could see clearly that her strengths connect her successes as her old 'work' self with what she has achieved as her current 'career break' self. Her conclusion is that, 'Perhaps I'm not a completely different person after all.' She thought about how she could use these strengths to help her along the journey back to work: 'I need to get more out there talking and making connections with new people who might be able to help me to find a job, rather than feeling stuck behind my laptop.'

Feel the fear

Mark had been in a senior role in government, coming out of a graduate programme into the Department of Trade, and spending fifteen years making his way up the ranks there. Three months after his second child was born, Mark started feeling discomfort in his chest when he exercised or walked up stairs, and was diagnosed with arrhythmia. 'With that on its own I might not have taken a break,' he says, 'but the kids were so little, and then my wife got a job overseas, so it made sense for me to take an extended "sabbatical" to support the family and try to get stronger again.' Three years later they moved back home, and Mark felt physically much fitter, and was keen to get back to work. He dusted off his CV and started researching jobs but, six months down the line and now over four years out of the workplace, he still hadn't applied for a single one. He hadn't even reached out to old colleagues for advice or leads, despite his network being very much still active.

Running through the coaching exercises already outlined, Mark doesn't have much trouble remembering his past achievements and connecting to his past self – in fact he has a folder full of material about past projects. And yet, he is full of doubt and worst-case scenarios. He feels unfulfilled, but he thinks his career break will be too big a hindrance to getting the kind of role he wants: 'Men are judged even more harshly for taking breaks. I don't want to put myself out there just to get rejected,' he says. He's also worried that his health issues will be another red flag for employers, as well as his career break.

What I see in Mark, and in many other talented people, is not simply a lack of confidence, but also fear. Or, more precisely, I see that fear underpins their lack of confidence: fear of failing, fear of looking stupid, fear of judgement, fear of rejection. Sometimes, too, a generalised fear that they won't be able to cope in a working world that's changed, or in the working world when they feel that they, themselves, have changed. I often hear fear in the 'what if' statements:

- 'What if I can't do what I did before?'
- 'What if I mess up the interview?'
- 'What if I can't get up to speed with the tech fast enough?'

In a strange way, it can be helpful to see that your lack of confidence is underpinned by a seemingly bigger issue: fear. That's because just trying to 'be more confident' can feel insurmountable, and lead to procrastination. But if you accept that you are to some degree afraid, you no longer have to wait for your confidence to (magically) appear in order to take the action you're hoping to take (sending that email, asking that person to lunch, applying for that job, for example). Instead, you can reframe confidence as courage. And the great news is that rustling up your courage to help you to take action, in spite of your self-doubts, often feels much more achievable than weaving confidence out of thin air.

Therefore, aim to summon a burst of courage. Decide to do something difficult, even though you feel afraid. We all have examples of a time when we've had to be brave. Thinking through a previous example with the 'Blueprint for courage' coaching exercise will give you a boost to do this again in a return-to-work context.

Self-coaching exercise: Create a blueprint for courage

Think about a time when you were afraid to try something new, but you took action anyway, and you succeeded at the new activity. It doesn't need to be something big.

Use the questions below to identify how you took the step to action, despite your fears, and then see if you can map some of the conclusions you've drawn here on to your next step in returning to work.

New activity

How did I prepare mentally to take action?

How did I prepare logistically?

What practice did I put in before starting?

Who and/or what helped me to keep going and succeed?

Implications for my return to work. How can I prepare/practise?
Who can I talk to before I leap in?

Mark went through the 'Blueprint for courage' exercise, focusing on successfully learning beginners' Japanese when the family relocated to Japan. He had initially procrastinated about taking lessons, worried that he would be useless at it and embarrass himself in front of a group of strangers. The thing that most helped him to summon up his courage was finding a friend, another expat, to go along with him to a trial class. They both stuck with it, using humour to quash their feelings of inadequacy when they struggled to make progress, and motivating each other not to give up. Thinking through that experience and how it might inform his actions now, Mark resolved to find a return-to-work buddy, to give him support as he gets going. 'My career break has shown me that I can try my hand at new things, at the same time as balancing all my other responsibilities. And that it's a lot easier with a bit of encouragement!'

Hopefully, by now you have reminded yourself of the things that you are truly good at and, even if you're not quite convinced yet of how much you have to offer, you are at least prepared to take a leap of courage. I want to come back now, for the final part of this chapter, to Ian Robertson's idea of confidence as a 'bridge to the future', that I introduced at the beginning of this chapter. As a reminder, this bridge combines 'can do' (a belief in your own abilities, which we've just worked to bolster) with 'can happen' (a belief that your abilities will lead to the desired outcome). In both parts, it is crucial to remember that your abilities, like your confidence, are not static. Do not look only at the past and present, but also to the future. If you believe in your ability to enhance and acquire new skills, those skills (and your confidence) will more easily follow.

Connect with what might be possible in the future – the growth mindset

How can we set ourselves up for success? Psychologist Carol Dweck, one of the world's leading authorities on motivation, has done a huge amount of research into this question. In her book, *Mindset*, she described the answer to be adopting a 'growth mindset'.

People with a 'fixed mindset' believe that intelligence is fixed, and that they don't have the capacity to change. If they have to work hard, or if they make mistakes, they take this as evidence of their lack of ability. This can lead to them avoiding challenges and staying in their comfort zone. In adults returning to work, a fixed mindset might show in confidence-battering thoughts such as: *I'm too old to learn something new, I'm hopeless with new technology* or *I'm no good at networking*.

People with a 'growth mindset', on the other hand, believe that intelligence can be continually developed. They view effort and hard work as ways to speed up their learning. They see mistakes as opportunities to learn and build new skills.

Embracing a growth mindset is powerful in your return to work: it propels you to move out of your comfort zone, to see the journey back as challenging rather than impossible, to stretch yourself in refreshing your skills and knowledge, to learn from setbacks and to persist despite setbacks to reach your goal.

Psychology: Growth mindset and achievement

Pioneering studies by Carol Dweck and her research teams have demonstrated the correlation between a growth mindset – the belief that intelligence can be continually developed – with higher academic achievement.

In one of the largest scale studies, Yeager, Dweck and colleagues studied 12,000 secondary school students from 65 US schools in the National Study of Learning Mindsets. One cohort of students participated in a short (less than one hour) online growth mindset intervention.

This focused on teaching them that intellectual abilities can be developed, using a memorable metaphor: that the brain is like a muscle that grows stronger and smarter with effort, with challenging work and with asking for help. Students were instructed to reflect on strategies to strengthen their brain through school work, and they were helped to internalise the concept by thinking how to teach this message to another pupil. This simple intervention led to sustained academic improvement for lower-achieving students, who were motivated to persist when hitting difficulties and motivated to take on harder learning experiences.

More recently, scientific studies into neuroplasticity (the ability of the brain to change its structure and organisation, both strengthening existing neural connections and forming new ones) have backed up the growth mindset concept. Researchers Lisa Pauwels and Eleonora Rossi have demonstrated that we can become increasingly skilled through effort and continued learning (see psychology box). What's more, we can improve our mental abilities at any age – neuroplasticity never stops.

Psychology: Neuroplasticity

Researchers used to believe that neurogenesis (the brain's creation of new neurons) stopped shortly after birth. As the saying goes: 'You can't teach an old dog new tricks.'

Today, we know that the brain is malleable, that it can reorganise pathways, create new connections and, at an extreme, birth new neurons in response to damage or as a result of learning.

These are two compelling studies on neuroplasticity:

1   Lisa Pauwels and colleagues trained young and old participants on a tracking task over three days, with a retention test six days later. They tested the levels of GABA (the neurotransmitter involved in brain plasticity) before and after training. Their results showed that GABA levels increased with training, even more so in older participants.

2   Eleonora Rossi and colleagues found that native English-speaking adults learning Spanish as a second language, experienced significant changes in the white matter of their brain. And the change didn't depend on how good they became at the language, it was the learning itself that was important.

Therefore, the theory that we can carry on learning throughout our lives is proven in multiple ways. Don't write yourself off as too old to learn new things. It's never too late!

How, then, can you actively embrace a growth mindset? There are some simple tactics you can try out in the coaching exercise below.

Self-coaching exercise: Adopt a growth mindset

Take your negative statements about what you can't do and re-frame them, using 'not yet'. This framing suggests that there is a challenge to be overcome, rather than an immovable barrier – an opportunity to develop new skills and acquire more experience.

What do I feel I can't do?	Reframe as 'not yet'
e.g. 'I'm hopeless with new technology'	Reframe: 'I'm not yet up to date with new technology'
e.g. 'I don't have a network any more'	Reframe: 'I'm not yet back in touch with my networks'

Challenge your belief that 'I'm too old to learn something new' with evidence. Remind yourself, using your notes from other exercises in this chapter, of all the many things you've learned so far, and believe that there are many more things you will learn in the future.

What new things have I learned in the past?

1

2

3

Start learning! Prove to yourself that you're not too old to learn something new by revisiting skills you feel out of practice with, or by taking steps to learn new ones. Take a tech updating course. Sign up for a course in a professional topic that appeals to you. You could also build your neuroplasticity by starting to learn another language or a musical instrument.

What new things appeal to me to learn now?

1

2

3

Back to Mark. His feeling is that his past achievements are all very well, but he's not up to date on current legal issues and the latest trade regulations. He thinks he will never be able to catch up. He is sure that he'll be rejected for the job he really wants, so there's no point applying, and therefore no point in signing up for courses that would bring his knowledge up to date. There is in here, of course, a lot of the negativity bias discussed in the last chapter (and a lot of fear mixed up with his lack of confidence). He does the 'Balance the scales' exercise (Chapter 1) to separate what is fact from what is belief. He goes away and finds some examples of people, including high-achieving men, who have returned to government roles after a similar length of break (for more about role models see Chapter 3, on self-efficacy). He comes around to the idea that 'there's stigma about men returning to work' is a belief that applies in some cases but is not a universal fact. He considers what practical steps these people might have taken to get back into the workplace and concedes that it is 'not impossible' to bring his knowledge and skills up to date.

This led naturally to the concept of 'not yet' – Mark accepted that he was 'not yet up to date' on current legal issues and the latest trade regulations. With encouragement from his new 'return-to-work buddy', he contacted two ex-colleagues to ask if they'd have a chat with him about recent trends and key changes during the last four years. He signed up to two updating courses, one online and one through a professional association. A month into the courses, and he was starting to feel less vulnerable about his knowledge gaps. He finally felt confident (or courageous!) enough to send out his first job application, to a position that one of his ex-colleagues had told him about.

Whichever ways you go about rebuilding your confidence, it is essential to remember that it can be a slow process, and confidence is not static. If you anticipate that your confidence will ebb and flow through your return-to-work journey, you'll be better placed to stave off a downturn. But remember, you cannot simply think your-self into confidence. You have to take action. Confidence follows action, not the other way around. The strategies in this chapter can help you warm up to the idea of taking the first step – but at some point you just need to take it. Make contact with an old colleague, call a recruiter for a chat, apply for that job you've been eyeing up (although do take a look through Chapters 5 to 7 first). Every small step that you take will accumulate until, over time, you are ready – and eager – to return to work.

Confidence is a huge topic, and we're not finished with it. In the next chapter, we'll pick up with another angle on confidence – self-efficacy: all to do with your belief in whether returning to work is possible. So far, we've been looking inwards. Now let's start to look outwards.

Summary

- A career break often negatively impacts your 'professional confidence' – your belief in yourself as a skilled, competent professional – even if it does not knock your *overall* confidence.
- Professional confidence is closely tied to professional identity.
- Start to regain your professional identity by reconnecting with the working person you used to be, recognising your core strengths as they are now, and considering what might be possible in the future. You have a USC, and there are exercises here to find it.
- Reframe confidence as courage and take a first step in spite of your fears.
- Adopt a 'growth mindset' and harness the power of 'not yet'.

'Believe in your ability. Back yourself. Keep saying "I do can it!" All the skills you have acquired, no matter how long ago, really *are* still there. And for every one thing that you might be slower at for now, there are three or four skills you are better at.' Rita, now back at work as a project manager in health services, after a six-year break

'Does anyone make it back to fulfilling work after so long?'

How to Believe That Getting Back – to the Right Job – is Even Possible

Way back, before I started Career Returners, eight women sat around my kitchen table. They had very different working backgrounds, from marketing to science to law, but they were united in two important ways. First: they were all experienced, skilled professionals who had taken a long career break for childcare. Second: they were all, now, starting to miss the professional aspect of their lives and thinking of adding work back in. Some wanted to pick up their careers where they left off, whereas others wanted to pivot in a new direction. They had joined me that day for a 'How to Get Back to Work' workshop that I was trialling, in the hope of supporting women on a career break in my local community.

Around the table, we talked about how isolated they felt, as they tried to picture a route back to fulfilling work. Most of them admitted that they didn't have friends who were also trying to re-launch their careers. Even pooling ideas and experiences between the eight of them, they could think of only a handful of people they knew who had made it back into the types of jobs they used to have after many years out.

> Janette said: 'I don't want just any job. I miss my old career. But I don't know anyone who's taken a long career break and is back in any sort of corporate job, apart from one friend who was recruited by her ex-boss. I just can't see that it's possible to get back to where I was, after I've been out for so long.'

> Mara added: 'I really want to get back into something to do with history. It was my degree subject and I loved it, but it is an area that I've never really worked in, as I went straight into finance. It's too late now, though, isn't it? No one would want to train up someone of my age.'

Even if you are sure you want to get back to a career (Chapter 1), and you feel that you are, in terms of your skills, strengths and mindset, capable of doing so (Chapter 2), you may still contemplate the twistiness of the path from here to there and decide that returning is an impossible goal. That belief, in itself, can stop you from even trying to make it happen.

From *can do* to *can happen* – build your sense of possibility

Let's go back again to Professor Robertson's explanation of confidence in Chapter 2: that it combines a 'can do' belief in your own abilities with a 'can happen' belief that your abilities will lead to the desired outcome. We covered 'can do' in the last chapter. Now we're going to tackle 'can happen'. The big question is: do you believe that the return you're aiming for, to fulfilling work that fits with your life, is fundamentally possible?

This is less about you and more about your perception of the world you're living in. The lack of a 'can happen' belief sounds like:

'Employers will always hire a fresh graduate over someone older like me who hasn't worked for nearly a decade.' Janette, pharmaceutical marketing manager, after an eight-year break

'I'll never get an interview with a big gap on my résumé.' Lara, history teacher, after a five-year break

'Technology moves too quickly now – I'll never be able to catch up.' Li, software developer, after a three-year break

'It's impossible to get a job when you're over 50.' Rahul, graphic designer, after a two-year break

'Working mothers always feel guilty, don't they? Even if I do get back, I'll probably be too stressed to enjoy it.' Petra, doctor, after a ten-year break

Psychologist Albert Bandura coined the term 'self-efficacy' to describe a person's belief in their ability to meet the challenges ahead and succeed at a given thing. This belief affects your feelings, your behaviour and – in the end – your likelihood of success.

High self-efficacy – believing you can succeed – gives you an incentive to take action. It also makes you more motivated to continue making progress, and to become more resilient, so that you can keep going through setbacks. The flipside, low self-efficacy, is a mindset within which you don't believe it's possible to succeed. You think that whatever you do, it won't make a difference – you won't get back to a great job. Your brain then looks for evidence that the barriers you encounter are insurmountable, reinforced by another mind-trap: confirmation bias – our tendency to look for and focus on information consistent with our beliefs. When you encounter a setback, you may well leap on it as evidence for your original belief that returning to a great job was unachievable. Then, you're more likely to give up or settle for less.

Consider Mara, above, whose plans were already, at this early stage, being affected by low self-efficacy: 'I'll never find anyone who'll pay to train me up, so I think I'll go for an admin job at my local college, that I can do with my eyes closed. It's better than nothing.' She's decided to settle for less than she wants, before she's even tried to aim higher.

Or Janette, who was wondering whether to bother trying to get back to her old sector, after an initial knockback: 'I spoke to a recruiter who told me I don't stand a hope of getting back into pharma and I should think about being a science teacher. He's probably right – it's been too long.'

How can you build your self-efficacy?

The good news is that self-efficacy is not fixed. You can build it up, if you understand how. Bandura identified four main ways to increase your self-efficacy: vicarious experiences, verbal persuasion, master experiences and emotional and physiological states. Simply put, they are:

1. Find role models
2. Get encouragement from other people
3. Refresh your skills
4. Manage your wellbeing

We will come back to these latter two points in later chapters. For now, at this building-blocks stage, it is the first two points that are important.

Find role models

For something to feel possible, we need to see that it is possible. We need people like us to observe and emulate. As the line goes, 'You can't be what you can't see.' However, what we often hear from returners, like Janette at the start of this chapter, is that they don't see any success stories. They don't see other people who took long breaks but have made it back to the kind of work they did before and who are thriving in their new roles. Instead, all they see around them are friends, ex-colleagues and family who have never taken a long break, or who are on a break but not showing much inclination to return to a career.

If they're not right in front of your nose, or immediately evident in your social circles, how can you build up a bank of motivating return-to-work success stories?

- **First, use your networks** Ask your friends and ex-colleagues if they know anyone who has returned to work in your field or a similar one, or who has made the career change you're considering. Professional associations in your sector may be able to help here too.
- **Second, get online** You can find a library of success stories on the Career Returners website and hear returners telling their stories of being back at work on the Career Returners Podcast. It's also worth looking at literature from big companies in your field – if they run returner or retraining programmes, they'll often feature their own case studies on their websites.

One last note on role models. Make sure, as you research, to look out for *relatable* role models. It's important that you see some part of yourself in their stories and that their achievements feel attainable from where you're standing. If your role models are too stellar (comparing yourself to a president or a tech CEO or an Olympic athlete, for example), you risk finding them demotivating rather than inspiring. Don't be demotivated if the initial examples you find don't have much in common with you. Keep looking until you find people who feel like you: perhaps they're a similar age, or have the same type of job, or had the same length of career break. Role models will only 'act as representations of the possible', and have a positive effect on your self-efficacy, if they feel relatable and attainable.

Psychology: Role models

Don't shoot too high with your role models, or it could backfire. Psychologist Leire Gartzia illustrated this in a 2021 study. She presented one group of PhD students with a profile of a successful post-doctoral researcher who was described as excellent but not exceptional, and the other group with a profile of a successful researcher who was described as exceptional. Those students who read about the excellent researcher expressed greater expectations of future success in academia and higher academic career intentions, than those who read about the exceptional researcher. The success of the excellent researcher was felt to be attainable, so their story acted as a motivating role model, whereas the success of the exceptional researcher was felt to be not attainable, so reading their story had a demotivating effect.

Get encouragement from other people – build your return-to-work support team

Most of us talk to other people when we're making important decisions or plans. Talking things through helps our ideas to become concrete and moves us towards action. Receiving encouragement from others helps to build our sense of possibility and to keep us motivated.

So, take a practical step to build your self-efficacy by creating a group of return-to-work supporters. First, identify and seek out your 'cheerleaders' among the people you know: those friends and family members who are encouraging and positive, and who fill you with a sense of possibility.

Second, build your return-to work support group. The aim is to partner with one or more people who are also looking to return to work, to help each other to stay motivated and to feel less isolated.

To find like-minded returners:

- Ask around your friendship group to see if anyone knows other people returning to work.
- Look for online communities of returners (such as the global Career Returners Community).
- Look for online communities relating to the reason for your career break (such as childcare, other caring, health, expat/ relocation).

I've seen the power of return-to-work support groups on numerous occasions. Janette, Mara and one of the other women from my first workshop formed naturally into a strong and supportive group, and they met regularly to keep each other on track. As Mara told me: 'These amazing women knew exactly how to help me pick myself up and keep going when I was losing hope that I would find a role to get excited about.'

Finding a return-to-work support team is particularly important if you're not getting the level of support you expect – and normally get – from the people you're closest to. These are some of the reactions returners have told me that they received from close friends and family when they talked about returning to work:

- 'What do you want to go back to work for? You're so lucky to be able to be at home.'
- 'Well, if you're absolutely sure that's what you want to do ...'

- 'If you think you can manage that and the family without getting too stressed ... All the working mothers I know are exhausted.'

These kinds of dispiriting comments can be a major blow to your feelings of self-efficacy. If you're facing comments like these, try not to take them at face value or see them as malicious. Bear in mind that those nearest and dearest to you may have a lot invested in maintaining the status quo. Your friends who are also on career break want to keep you on their 'team' – they don't want to lose you to the workplace! And your plans to return to work might make them question or feel insecure about their own decisions. Your family may have got used to the arrangements and routines established during your break, and might feel anxious about upsetting the balance, or about extra responsibilities falling on their own shoulders. To dig even deeper into some psychology: the people who know you best will tend to define you by the role they're used to seeing you in, and they will struggle to see you in a new light.

A caveat: belief vs reality

Self-efficacy, of course, can take you only so far. This isn't a fantasy world where a positive view of the future is the only thing that determines your success. I'm not denying the existence of very real environmental and societal factors that can get in the way of your return to a great job. In recruitment, there is ageism, similarity bias (when interviewers lean towards candidates that feel the most like themselves), and bias against candidates without recent experience. Plus, once you're back at work, there are far too many inflexible roles and overly demanding employers.

We'll talk about these again in Chapter 7. What I want to say now, though, is that these barriers and biases aren't universal. Many employers value candidates that can bring maturity, experience and diversity to their teams. Some employers even specifically target returners. And many workplaces are now far more flexible in terms of when and where you work.

My core message to finish off is that while it might be hard to get back to a fulfilling role, it *is* possible. And if you can fundamentally believe this, you're much more likely to aim high, start positively, keep going through obstacles, and eventually land back where you want to be.

Summary

- People with high self-efficacy – the belief that it is possible to succeed – are more likely to achieve their goals.
- To believe something is possible, you need to see it. Seek out relatable role models: examples of people like you who have made it back to fulfilling work after a long break.
- Build your return-to-work support team – and recognise that you may have to look beyond your close friends and family to find your cheerleaders.

'Surround yourself with as much positivity as possible. Don't believe all those people who tell you it's not possible to get back, or that it's too late to do something different. There is a world of opportunities out there for you!' Mara, now back at work as a business manager in a heritage conservation organisation after a five-year break

4

'What do I want to do next?'

Setting Your Career Compass

You've made lots of mental progress since those 'shall I, shan't I' early morning worries. You're sure you want to go back to work, and you're starting to feel confident (sometimes less, sometimes more) about it. Deciding what you actually want to do next, however, is not always simple. Do you go back to what you did before, do you use your skills in a related area, or do you branch out into a completely new field?

This is big decision-making – and it might feel knotty. It's also an amazing opportunity! This is likely to be the first time for a very long time – perhaps even since leaving school – that you've had the chance to think about what you really want to do with your working life. It's a perfect moment to step back, take stock and then move forward with renewed motivation and a clearer view about what you want from your next chapter.

Consider these two returners, trying to decide what to do next:

Ana started her career as a market analyst in the mining sector. She found the work 'quite interesting' but was never comfortable in the male-dominated environment: she hated being the only woman in meetings and was often excluded from social activities after work. When her partner was posted overseas with the army, she felt largely relieved to leave her job to go with him. Over the next ten years they lived in six countries, never for more than two years at a time. Ana picked up local jobs where she could – her favourite was as an administrator at a local school – before taking a full career break when they had their two children. Now, twelve years on, the family is finally settled back in her home country and she desperately wants to get back to a career. She's sure that she doesn't want to go back to mining, and she's excited about a career change. She has been looking at retraining as a nutritionist, as she's become really interested in food and nutrition during her career break, but she is worried about the time and the cost, and generally whether it's the right move.

Mia's dilemma is a bit different. She loved the excitement of working as a City lawyer. Having worked so hard to qualify, she was devastated when a cancer diagnosis forced her to take a career break. Now, in remission and after nearly five years out, she dreams of going back to law, but she feels, physically and mentally, still fragile. She cannot imagine slogging through the same commute and hours and stress that she did before. Really, she can't see that it's possible to work as a corporate lawyer with less intensity than she did before – but she thinks that working for a local firm would be too much of a step down. Even with those things in mind, she is finding it hard to give up on the idea of resuming her legal career.

How do you decide what to do next? Perhaps, like Ana, you never really connected with your previous career and you're keen to do something that feels like a better fit. Or perhaps, like Mia, you loved your job and would like to pick up where you left off, but you can't imagine being able to work the way you did before.

Whatever your situation, this chapter will give you a framework to start to move forward again. That framework is your internal 'career compass'. Your compass will give you a direction to set off in and should, further down the line, help you to steer a course beyond a destination that is too vague ('something in tech'/'something with people'/'an interesting part-time job') without landing you at one that is overly narrow and inflexible ('programme manager in a big tech firm').

To help you set your own career compass, I'll guide you through a two-stage process:

1. First, we will create your one-page 'self-snapshot: who I am and what I want', identifying the key elements that will make a job both fulfilling for you and a good fit with your life at this stage.
2. Then, based on this snapshot, in Chapter 5 we will develop your return-to-work decision criteria, to help you generate and prioritise a manageable number of energising job options, that you can then reality test.

More so than in previous chapters, we're now going to get quite workbook-like and into the nitty-gritty. Get ready to jot down your ideas. There is a series of self-coaching exercises coming, and it is best to work through them all in order if you want to end up with a complete and honest snapshot and set of criteria. A warning: you might find yourself getting frustrated with this introspective stage and therefore make excuses to skip straight through to the action steps. We often see this happening with people who don't enjoy self-analysis, who put themselves at the bottom of the family priority pile, or who feel an urgent financial pressure to get back to work. However, if you're focused and don't procrastinate, this process doesn't need to take too long – it can be worked through in a few weeks rather than a few months. And, whatever your pace, I can assure you that taking the time now will really pay off. It'll help you to feel more confident in your career decision-making and to be more targeted and effective in your job search.

Find job fulfilment

Before we dive into creating your self-snapshot, I'd like to talk about your primary goal here: finding fulfilment at work. I deliberately don't talk about finding work that 'makes you happy' – happiness is a temporary emotion, so it will ebb and flow. Indeed, seeking happiness can conversely make you less happy (see psychology box below).

Fulfilment is a longer-lasting state of being, so is more achievable and sustainable. Positive psychology has delved into what makes us feel fulfilled in life. Psychologist Martin Seligman calls this 'flourishing'. There are many different aspects (see psychology box below), but in the context of our career self-reflection, three core drivers stand out:

1. **Using your strengths** To echo the last chapter, you need to be good at, and energised by, what you're doing, to be engaged and have a sense of achievement.
2. **Being in line with your values** Your work needs to feel important to you, to give you a sense of purpose and meaning.

3. **Being linked with your interests** You need to be interested in what you do, to get a sense of enjoyment, pleasure and engagement.

Psychology: Happiness and flourishing

On happiness, why does psychology research suggest that happiness is not a wise career goal? According to four studies reported by Kim and Maglio in 2018, people who pursue happiness as a goal ironically can become less happy rather than more. In one of these studies, Mauss and colleagues found that happiness-seekers often feel more time-constrained and pressured, reducing their sense of contentment.

On flourishing, Martin Seligman, the pioneer of positive psychology, has spent many years studying what makes our lives more fulfilling. His 2001 PERMA model summarises the research findings into five core elements that enable us to 'flourish' and get the most out of life: **P**ositive emotions, **E**ngagement, **R**elationships, **M**eaning and **A**ccomplishment. This is a useful framework to consider what makes work fulfilling for you. Here's my take on the five elements, with related questions to ask yourself in relation to your past and future career:

1   Doing things that bring you enjoyment and pleasure. Does your work make you feel good?
2   Being absorbed and fully engaged in the activities you pursue. Are you applying your strengths?

---

3 Having deep, meaningful connections with others. Do you have good working relationships with your colleagues?

4 Having a sense of purpose. Do you feel that what you do is important?

5 Realising your goals. Do you have a sense of achievement in your work?

It might be tempting, when you see these core components – strengths, values and interests – to leap to online personality assessments to tell you 'who you are' and 'what you want'. There can be a place for these down the line, but they're not a magic tool that will give you the 'right' answer. Taking time to look inward with some structured reflection will give you a much deeper understanding of yourself in relation to work. This is where your age is a huge asset. Your life to date, in and out of work, has been filled with positive and negative experiences. This gives you a whole heap of raw material from which to draw evidence, to shine a light on what you like and don't like, what energises you and what's important to you – to pull out meaningful threads and themes.

To create your self-snapshot, we're going to look at six core components, building towards the answer to these important questions:

1. What are my strengths?
2. What are my values?
3. What are my interests?
4. What are my motivations?

5. What do I need/want to earn?
6. How do I want/need to work?

We'll focus on each of these components in turn. At the end, I will talk about how to summarise them into your self-snapshot and to use them together to develop your return-to-work decision criteria.

What are my strengths?

In Chapter 2 we looked at your strengths in order to help rebuild your confidence. Your strengths are also a fundamental building block for your career decision-making. Studies show that if you orientate your career around using your strengths, you are likely to be more satisfied, more engaged and perform better.

Therefore, go back to the self-coaching exercise where you pulled out your top three strengths, 'Finding my USC (unique strengths combination)' on page 51. These will form the first segment of your self-snapshot. Don't forget the detail, or you might set off down the wrong track. For example, one returner, an ex-accountant, joined an accounting recruitment business because she'd decided that one of her core strengths was 'working with people'. 'I was talking to people all day long, but I didn't find it energising at all. I realised that what I love is collaborating with a team of people on new projects, not interviewing and assessing them.' The more specific you are, the easier it will be to point yourself towards job options that truly use your strengths and enable you to thrive.

What are my work values?

We talk a lot these days about finding work that fits with your values, but what does that actually mean? In daily life, we tend to use 'values' to mean core beliefs and ways of living, such as honesty and kindness. But in career psychology and coaching, values are defined far more broadly. They are simply the factors that are most important to you in your working life. They do relate to what makes work meaningful to you and may reflect that same sense of moral attribute, such as 'integrity', but they can also (such as 'autonomy' or 'having a high-status job') have nothing to do with that everyday 'core belief' definition.

Our values often change with age and experience. Take a moment here to consider if yours have shifted during your career break. It can be tricky to identify your values in a vacuum, so we'll use the work values coaching exercise below to get you going.

Self-coaching exercise: My work values

Look at the following list of some commonly occurring values. Tick all the values that are important to you to any extent. Be honest with yourself. There are no better or worse values, so don't self-edit to end up with a list of values that you think sound better than the others, or a list of values you would like to have rather than those that you actually have. If you have one or more important values that aren't on the list, add them under 'other'. Leave aside flexible working or financial reward for now, as we'll pick those up later.

Security and stability
To feel financially secure. To have security of employment. To have low risk.

Expertise
To be an expert in my area. To apply and develop my skills in a particular area of knowledge. To be acknowledged as an expert.

Recognition
To be recognised for my achievements. To get positive feedback for good work.

Influence and leadership
To influence the thoughts and actions of others. To lead other people. To be responsible and accountable for organisational results.

Creativity and innovation
To have the opportunity to be innovative and imaginative. To develop and create new ideas. To create my own enterprise.

Independence and autonomy
To decide how I spend my time. To have a high degree of control over what I do. To make my own decisions.

Integrity
To be true to my own ideals and beliefs. To work for an employer with integrity.

Self-development
To have the opportunity for continued personal and professional growth. To learn new skills and knowledge.

Pure challenge
To engage in complex and
demanding tasks. To put my abilities
to the test. To be intellectually
challenged. To solve difficult
problems.

Relationships
To have close relationships with
colleagues. To belong to a team.
To work in a supportive environment.

Societal benefit
To make the world a better place
to live. To help others and make a
difference.

Variety
To have considerable variety of
activity. To have considerable variety
of people.

Position and status
To have a senior position and job
title. To work for a prestigious
employer.

Developing other people
To help other people develop and
grow. To coach or mentor others.

Other [add any of your values that
are missing.]

Now establish your top three values. Prioritise by considering what
trade-offs you would be prepared to make if you found a great job,
and which things are the fundamentals on which you would not
compromise. If you are struggling to prioritise, rank your entire set
of important values so that you are forced to put them in an order.

Get more specific, by thinking about what your top three values mean to you. Use the descriptive phrases from the list to help you. For example:

1   By creativity, you might mean you want to:
    • Practically express your artistic side.
    • Be in an environment where your creative ideas are welcome.

2   By independence and autonomy, you might mean you want to:
    • Have total freedom over your working life, to set the strategy and deliver on it.
    • Have a strong degree of independence of action within a strategic framework set by others.

3   By status you might mean you want:
    • A job title that is widely recognisable, such as 'partner' or 'creative director'.
    • To be managing a team of at least X people.

Top 3 values

1:

For me, this means ...

2:

For me, this means ...

3:

For me, this means ...

What are my interests?

The third core component of job fulfilment is doing something that interests you.

There are two sides to interests: (1) the activities you enjoy doing (2) the topics that you're drawn to. You may find, as with your values, that both have evolved considerably during your career break. This is a good moment to consider whether any of your interests (whether longstanding or more recent) could develop into a new career option, or whether you'd prefer to keep them as hobbies rather than bringing them into your working life. Get your thinking cap on again, as there are two coaching exercises to work through here.

Self-coaching exercise: My ideal work day

1. Think of each of your past roles as a series of building blocks based on the activities those roles involved, such as meeting with clients, analysing data or samples, recruiting, coaching, writing, researching, presenting, designing. If you're struggling to think of activities, think verbs!

2. For each role, write down all the activities you did, either regularly or occasionally.

   Repeat the exercise for the roles you've taken up during your career break, such as volunteering, running a home business, or studying.

3. Look at all the activities you've listed and underline the three or four you most enjoyed and would put together to create

your ideal work day. A good test is whether you feel energised when you think about a day like this.

Past work or career break role	What activities did this role involve?

Self-coaching exercise: Appealing topics

This is a free-flowing exercise. Write down whatever comes into your head when you read the prompt questions in the table below. Now look at your answers and think: could they be relevant from a future career perspective? You may be sure that 'local history', 'psychology', 'cycling', 'theatre' or 'nutrition' are just hobbies, but perhaps there is something there worth considering in a work context. Underline one or two interests from this list that you would like to explore incorporating into your working life.

Question	Answer	Potentially work-related?
What magazines/non-fiction books/podcasts am I drawn to?		
What types of article catch my eye when I'm reading a newspaper or journal?		
What have I studied, or what hobbies have I pursued, purely for pleasure?		
What topic would I most enjoy giving a short talk to other people about?		

What are my motivations?

In Chapter 1, you laid out your top three motivations for returning to work (page 32). Pull those out, as they will be the input for the fourth segment of your self-snapshot. You may find that they overlap with your values – that's OK, it just reinforces how important they are.

Your motivations provide essential 'must-have' material for your decision criteria. For example, if one of your motivations is the social side of working, think twice about taking on a solitary role, such as a solo project or consulting role, even if that fits with the flexibility you want. Or if one of your motivations is mental stimulation, taking on a role which is well below your skills level – that you could do 'with your eyes closed' – is unlikely to be satisfying.

What you have gathered so far are the internal components of the self-snapshot: looking inward at you as a person. Now it's time to look outward – at your environment and the logistics of a potential job – focusing in on the key areas of pay, flexibility and any other practical constraints such as location, health management and the ability to travel.

What do I need/want to earn?

Financial considerations are at the top of the list for many returners and are captured in the fifth element of your self-snapshot. Money, or more accurately the lack of it, can be a major stumbling block when you're looking at going back to work. If you're considering a flexible job, or shorter hours, and particularly if you are starting again in a new field, you may find the salaries offered are considerably lower than the salary you netted before your break. If you're a working parent, childcare costs can eat a huge chunk of your income. Once you add it all up, it feels easiest to decide it's not worth your while going back at all.

The best thing you can do, initially, is take the emotion out of the equation, to decide what you need to earn. There's an important point to remember here if you have a partner, and (as for most returners) your motivations to return go beyond the financial. Household and family costs are a shared expense, so financial trade-offs and decisions need to be made by looking at total household income and expenses, not just yours.

Once you've looked at your needs, bring the emotion back in to consider what you want to earn. This might be based on what you previously earned: you might be strongly averse to accepting a drop in salary, and it's important to acknowledge those feelings. Or it may be about getting a mid-/high-market rate for the roles you're targeting. This is not just about ego. Working for less than you feel you deserve can chip away at your self-esteem, your pride and your sense of being valued – so you need to feel that you're paid what you're worth.

While acknowledging your sense of worth, I do encourage you to remain open to exciting roles with opportunities for growth. Remind yourself that you have more leeway with the salary you want to earn than with the salary you need.

Self-coaching exercise: My financial needs and wants

Calculate what you need to earn, using the table below as a prompt.

Return-to-work costs	Monthly	Annual
Travel		
Work clothes		
Childcare/carer		
Cleaner/other household costs		
Other costs:		
Other costs:		

Total itemised costs		
10 per cent margin for unexpected costs		
Total break-even cost to return to work	A	
Expenses to fund:		
Housing costs (mortgage, etc.)		
Family costs (schooling, etc.)		
Other costs:		
Other costs:		
Total expenses to fund	B	
Salary I need to earn	A+B	

Now decide what you want to earn.

Previous salary	
Current market salary range	
Salary I want to earn (range)	

In which way do I want/need to work?

We're now moving on to the final component of the self-snapshot. The world of work has changed a lot in recent years. Remote working and hybrid working (a mix of work on business premises and from home) have become much more normal, rather than the exceptions they used to be. Many jobs now involve much less travel, because meetings can be held virtually. However, this varies by employer, sector and country, so you'll need to do your research to find out what your options are. I'll talk later about how to handle asking a prospective employer for your preferred working patterns. For now, let's establish what kind of work will actually work for you.

Flexibility

It's no surprise that returners – who so often have young children, continuing caring responsibilities or health issues – tend to put 'flexible working' at the top of their wish list. This can also come as a by-product of the perspective gained from your career break. You may now be looking for a way of working that challenges and fulfils you, without running you into the ground.

My key advice is to be open minded about the type of flexibility that can work for you. Many returners, needing greater work–home balance, focus on part-time as the only way to go, become fairly rigid in a quest for a three- or four-day week, and massively limit their options in the process. Apart from a few countries, we're not yet in a world where there is an abundance of part-time professional roles.

To broaden your options, consider whether a full-time role could work for you, if you have more control or flexibility around where and when you work. Instead of starting with a working pattern that you assume you want, start with what you want to use the flexibility for, and then consider a pattern around that. Look at the 'Types of flexible working' table below. Whether you're a parent and you want to do the school run, you're managing a chronic health condition, or you need to fit in visits to an elderly relative, could flexible start/finish times and/or remote or hybrid working be a solution? If you want to be around during school holidays, could extended or unpaid holiday leave cover this?

Self-coaching exercise: Types of flexible working

These are some of the most common forms of flexible working – think about which could work for you.

Part-time working	Less than five days a week
Flexible start or finish times	You can start earlier and finish earlier, or vice versa. You may agree to work specific core hours, with flex around these times
Remote working	Working from home or other remote location
Hybrid working	Working part of the time in the office or on-site and part of the time remotely
Extended or unpaid holiday/vacation leave	Having extended annual leave or an agreement to take a certain amount of unpaid leave annually (often used to cover school holidays)
Term-time hours	Only working school term times
Compressed hours	Working a full-time week across a shorter period (a four-day week or a nine-day fortnight), with longer hours on the working days
Annualised hours	Contractually working a certain number of days in the year, with a flexible agreement to work when it suits you and the business

I've seen many returners be pleasantly surprised that they can get the work–life balance they need in a full-time flexible role. My key message is: be flexible about flexibility!

Location, travel and other constraints

Finally, consider any other constraints. For example, do you have family or personal commitments that fix you to a certain location and restrict the amount of travel you can do? Do you have other accommodations that you need for your health?

Put some notes together on your ideal working patterns and constraints. You now have the sixth and final part of your self-snapshot.

Self-coaching exercise: Self-snapshot – who I am and what I want

Use the previous exercises in this chapter to complete this table

1 What are my strengths?	2 What are my values?
3 What are my interests?	4 What are my motivations?
5 What do I need/want to earn?	6 Which way do I want/need to work?

When you look at your self-snapshot, what you see on the page is an emerging picture of who you are, and what you want out of work for this next stage of your life. You'll notice that there is nothing even close to a job description here – this is a picture of you, not of a role. What you might start to notice too, though, are overlaps between the sections. Themes and repetitions. These will be good threads to start to pull on.

Back to Ana. She worked as a market analyst in mining, but she didn't really like it, then she gave that up when she lived overseas for ten years, picking up a variety of 'random' jobs during that time, and now, back home and looking to start work in something different, she is thinking about being a nutritionist. Ana found, once she started these exercises, that the sheer variety of jobs she'd done before and during her break was really helpful – she had so much raw material to draw from. She recognised that she'd enjoyed tackling every relocation very analytically, researching and planning each step ('Perhaps being an analyst is my thing, after all'). She also saw that the volunteer roles she'd most enjoyed were working with a group rather than on her own. She gravitates towards the food section of the newspaper and has become fascinated by the links between diet and wellbeing. This interest started when she was exploring how to support one of her children with his mental health, and it had developed through reading around the topic and taking a few free online courses. 'It's definitely what I'd most like to talk to a group about – it's not exactly mining is it!' she says. This is what Ana put together as her self-snapshot:

Self-snapshot – Ana's example

1 What are my strengths?	2 What are my values?
Collaborating with others to reach a goal Adaptability Research and analysing information	Belonging to a team Variety of activity Making a difference to individuals
3 What are my interests?	4 What are my motivations?
Activities: mapping out ideas with a team, learning about innovations, researching and analysing Interests: nutrition, culture, health	Intellectual stimulation Regaining my professional identity Social side
5 What do I need/want to earn?	6 Which way do I need/want to work?
Need: [To be calculated] Want: [analyst role] a mid-level market rate salary, not a graduate salary, to reflect my experience/ [career change] need to cover costs of retraining course	Flexibility to be home by 6 p.m. and attend important school events No unplanned travel

You may want to turn your self-snapshot into a visual image, or a mind map. It can look any way you want it to, as long as it resonates with you.

You're nearly there on setting your career compass! Now you need to take the picture you've drawn of yourself, and turn it into a powerful job search tool. You do that by translating your snapshot into a list of decision criteria – you'll then have a set of criteria against which you can weigh up potential return-to-work options.

Self-coaching exercise: My return-to-work decision criteria

Using your self-snapshot, complete the following table.

As you write each statement, think about how you can assess whether a particular job might meet those criteria. If the answer is not immediately obvious, add a sub-statement to make it more testable or more concrete (for example 'regaining my professional identity' could be testable by 'feeling proud of my job title'). Don't agonise too much about crafting perfect criteria or perfect tests – think of this as a first draft that you will revise as you move on to, and through, active exploration (Chapter 5). If you see that aspects of your list overlap, star them to group together into one criterion – see Ana's example below.

I'm looking for a job which …

Uses my strength of
Uses my strength of
Uses my strength of
Fits with my value of
Fits with my value of
Fits with my value of
Meets my motivations of
Includes the activity of
Includes the activity of

Includes the activity of

Relates to my interests of

Has a salary of [salary I need] to [salary I want]

Has flexibility to

Meets my other requirement(s) of

Return-to-work decision criteria – Ana's example
I'm looking for a job which … (example)

Uses my strength of collaborating with others (1)*

Uses my strength of adaptability (2)

Uses my strength of researching and analysing information (2)

Fits with my value of belonging to a team (1)

Fits with my value of variety of activity

Fits with my value of making a difference to individuals

Meets my motivations of regaining my sense of professional identity/ intellectual stimulation/social side (1)

Includes mapping out ideas with a team (1)

Includes learning about innovations

Includes researching and analysing (2)

Relates to nutrition, health, (perhaps) culture

Salary: Need [TBC]. Want: [analyst] mid-range salary; cover costs if retraining

Has flexibility to be home by 6 p.m. and attend important school events

No unplanned travel

*Notes: (1) Group together under working closely with a team? (2) Group under researching and analysing new topics?

Have a first go at prioritising your criteria by highlighting your 'must-haves': your non-negotiables. You're separating them from your 'nice-to-haves': the criteria where you could compromise for the right opportunity. If you have multiple overlaps in one area, that area will usually be one of your must-haves. You'll refine this prioritisation in the job-exploration phase, so think of this as a hypothesis to test rather than as set in stone.

Your decision criteria form your personal career compass. You'll use them to guide you through the decision-making process, towards a fulfilling job.

Fulfilment – the magnetic north for your compass

A final thought and tool for this chapter, to bear in mind as you move forward. What you have created with your decision criteria is a wish list. The concept of a 'dream job' that ticks every box, is perfectly crafted just for you, is – as the name suggests – both unrealistic and rarely realised. In the vast majority of cases, there will be compromises to be made. If you get into perfectionist mode and try to get everything all at once, you are likely to be looking for a very, very long time!

You might find it hard to prioritise one criterion over another, or struggle to accept any compromises on the working patterns or the salary you want. This is the time to remind yourself (from Chapter 1) that compromise is not a negative or a failure, it's an inevitable by-product of having a full life. Think about your life as a whole, and what trade-offs you could make, to ensure that a role works across all fronts – work, home and life more generally. You won't be aiming for 100 per cent in all these areas, rather 'just enough' of each.

To the question of what is most important, I've created the simple image of a 'Trade-off triangle' (diagram below) as a tool for considering return-to-work compromises. The three points of the triangle mark the broad factors that people are typically looking for in a role: job fulfilment, flexibility and a certain level of pay. I find that many returners make the mistake of starting with the flexibility they want – such as part-time work or locally based work – then look for jobs that fit with that. This too often ends up with them taking a role that is way below their skill and experience level, which can quickly lead to frustration.

The trade-off triangle

Job fulfilment

Flexibility   Pay/level

I've seen a much higher level of return-to-work success when returners focus first of all on what will make a job satisfying and rewarding for them. That's why, in the 'Trade-off triangle', fulfil-ment is positioned at the top – to symbolise that it needs to be the magnetic north for your career compass.

When you return to work, life gets busier and more complex. If you're not enjoying it, and you're drained by it rather than energised, it usually doesn't pan out in the long term, however highly you're paid or however flexible the job is. But if you enjoy it – if you feel energised, motivated and proud of what you're doing – you're more likely to feel happy and satisfied, and to stick with it.

To prioritise the factors that will make a job fulfilling for you, consider first what fits best with your strengths, interests, values and motivations (the first four segments of your self-snapshot). Then move on to how can you do this type of work flexibly and with the level of pay you need/want (the final two segments).

Now that you have your self-snapshot and a first draft of your prioritised decision criteria, let's use them in the next chapter to identify and explore exciting potential paths. For all of us, there are a number of possible routes we could take that will lead to satisfying and fulfilling work. And there is, I'm sure, a good option waiting for you.

Summary

- Your career break has given you an amazing opportunity: the chance to think about what you really want to do with your working life.
- Fulfilment is a more achievable goal than happiness at work.
- Put together a 'self-snapshot' including your strengths, values, interests and motivations (which all point to fulfilment at work), alongside some information about how you want to work, and how much you need and want to earn.
- Translate that self-snapshot into a set of decision criteria to assess return-to-work options.
- Make job fulfilment the magnetic north of your career compass.

'See your career break as an amazing window of opportunity – to think about who you are now and who you want to be in the working environment, to focus on what you can add to the workplace, as well as to work out what fits with your new life.'
Ana, now back at work as a market research analyst (part-time) and nutrition student (part-time), after a twelve-year break

PART II

FINDING WORK THAT WORKS

'Where do I start?'

How to Take the First Steps in Your Return-to-Work Job Search

You've come a long way on your return-to-work journey. You've bolstered your confidence and sense of possibility, you've dug deep into some self-reflection, and you have a clearer sense of direction, with an outline of your career 'must-haves' and 'nice-to-haves'. Now, you feel ready to move to the next stage exploring what jobs are out there. But you sit down at your computer and . . . you're drawing a blank. You've hit post-career break decision paralysis!

You may be like Jo, struggling to think what options might fit your criteria. 'It sounds stupid, but I've absolutely no idea what to do next. I know I don't want to go back to what I was doing – and opportunities in my old field are few and far between, anyway. I would love to find my "passion": the sort of work that gives my life meaning. Like that saying, "find something you love to do and you'll never have to work a day in your life". It feels like my last chance to do that. But how do I work out what my passion is?'

Or you may, like Naomi, have too many ideas, with paths forking away in all directions, 'I'm just going around in circles – no shortage of inspiration, but no idea what would be best for me and make me happy.' Too much introspection can wear you out, giving you an overwhelming urge to leap straight into applying for the first ten jobs you see advertised. As Naomi contemplated, 'I think I'll just start applying for any jobs I'm qualified for and see where it gets me.'

In this chapter, I'm going to help you to get past this decision paralysis. I'll guide you to use your self-snapshot and decision criteria to generate and assess career options. I then strongly encourage an 'active exploration' stage – the testing out of a few energising pathways – so that you can positively and realistically commit to your next step.

No ideas at all/too few ideas – how to generate job ideas

Jo had been in TV production before her career break. Having started her career full of energy and enthusiasm, she'd found it increasing stressful and in the end she hit burnout. She took a sabbatical to go travelling and then had two close family bereavements, which kept her out of work for another year. There are few opportunities in her old field and she's ready for a career change. But she's waiting for the perfect job to magically materialise, to make the path clear for her. I aimed to take Jo away from the concept of 'finding her passion', because it was keeping her stuck. In line with psychologist Paul O'Keefe's research (see psychology box below), I encouraged her to set the bar at a more realistic level: to reset her search as one for options she finds interesting and energising to explore.

Psychology: Growth mindset and interests

The often-proposed idea of 'finding your passion' is un-helpful when getting back to work. It suggests that your passion is out there, fully formed, waiting to be discovered. In fact, psychologist Paul O'Keefe, who has extensively researched the science of interest, has found that passions are not fixed and inherent. They can be cultivated and develop over time: you start with a spark of interest, then invest to build your knowledge and engagement in that in-terest, and reinforce the interest with positive experiences. In this way, the interest may transform into a passion.

O'Keefe, Dweck and Walton explored theories of interest in five studies. Building on Dweck's concept of growth mindsets discussed in Chapter 2 (page 61), they demonstrated that people who believe interests are fixed (a 'fixed mindset') are less open-minded about exploring new topics than those who believe interests can grow (a 'growth mindset'), and that a fixed mindset can lead you to have unrealistic expectations and to be less resilient in the face of setbacks. In one of the studies, arts students were given a science-focused article to read, and then their interest levels were rated. Those with a fixed mindset were less interested than those with a growth mindset.

The finding was repeated with science students reading an arts-focused article.

The researchers also found evidence that mindsets can be changed. In another of the five studies, participants read one of two articles: one claiming that interests are fixed and the other claiming that interests are flexible. Participants then watched a video on the theory of black holes and, if they remained interested, read a denser article on the topic. Those who had read about the fixed theory were more likely, after reading the denser article, to rate their interest levels as lower than those who had read about growth theory.

To help her to expand her job horizons, we got creative. I prompted Jo to involve some friends in brainstorming the sort of job she might want (see exercise below).

Self-coaching exercise: Job wanted brainstorm

Use your decision criteria to draw up an advert for the job you want. If you're the creative type, you could draw this instead of using a table. Thanks to Career Counselling Services for inspiring this exercise.

Job Wanted!

Skills I can offer:

1

2

3

The role characteristics I want:

1

2

3

The company characteristics I want:

1

2

3

Ask a few creative friends to join you for a job brainstorming session. Talk them through your job-wanted advert and invite them to ask questions. Now spend fifteen minutes on a job brainstorm where your friends offer ideas and you write them down. All ideas are welcome, and you are not allowed to critique them (be ready to bite your tongue, as this is easier said than done!). At the end, underline all the options that you think could be interesting. Now put a star next to the three that you feel most energised about exploring, and note them here:

The three most energising ideas

Option 1
Option 2
Option 3

Exercise variants: if this feels daunting, or the friends you want to involve live far away, you can email your advert to your friends and ask them to send back three to five job ideas. You can also tap into AI tech to generate ideas based on your job advert.

Job wanted! – Jo's example

Full time, with flexible hours and hybrid working
(at least 2 days remote working)

Salary range: XX-YY

Skills offered:
Creativity a must - an 'ideas person'
Strong project management skills
Influencing skills

About the role:
Working within a small team, with a high degree of autonomy and with clear pathways for progression

About the company:
A wider ethical focus, social purpose and innovative culture

The advert reminded Jo a little of the volunteer job she'd taken during the past year – as a community fundraiser – so she wrote that down as an option to explore. She'd dismissed it before only because she didn't think of it as a potential paid career option.

She then set up the brainstorming session with three creative friends who were happy to help. When they asked her if she was prepared to retrain (for example as a graphic designer), she decided that she couldn't afford to spend money on lengthy courses, so she would only consider options if they used her transferable skills, where she could access free courses or where she was paid to train.

At the end of the brainstorm they had filled a large sheet of paper with ideas. Jo underlined all the options that she thought could be interesting to explore. She was excited to see seven possibilities, ranging from 'fundraising in an innovative charity' to '(funded) retraining into AI'.

She expanded her list by using online search terms relating to her self-snapshot. She searched under 'careers using innovative thinking' and came up with a few additional jobs that appealed. She also used an AI tool, putting in the types of roles she was interested in and asking for different ideas.

Other approaches might work for you

There are variants on this jobs brainstorm that you can use, even if you start from a more specific place.

Remember Mia from the last chapter? She knew that she wanted to pick up her legal career again, but in a way that gave her a better work–life balance. She felt a bit nervous about the group brainstorm, so she decided that she would prefer to get written options from a wider range of people. She emailed her key decision criteria to a mix of friends with legal and non-legal backgrounds and asked them to suggest 'flexible roles in law' that could be a fit for her. She collated all the responses on to one page. As the page filled up with options, she realised that she had been too black and white about law, seeing her choice as either an exciting but overly demanding role like she did before, or a dull but manageable local law role. Now she started to see other options, such as working as an associate for a flexible legal outsourcing firm, that could be viable for her. She also got excited by a few ideas on how she could do a career pivot, to use her legal skills in a related area, such as regulation or mediation.

Too many ideas

Naomi has also been thinking a lot about her next step. Having previously liked ('but not loved') her role as a customer relationship manager for a prestigious bank, she feels that she's changed a huge amount during her ten-year career break. She feels she has new motivations, perspectives and interests. She's put a huge amount of thought into deciding her 'best' return-to-work career option – two years' worth of thought, in fact. In that time, she's come up with eighteen ideas and has researched each one in depth, collecting information in neatly labelled folders. She's done a variety of psychometric assessments which have each pointed her towards a totally different job that would be her 'best fit'. And now it's January again, another year gone. 'I'm really annoyed with myself. I'm no closer to getting back to work than I was last year. In fact, I feel even further away from deciding on the best way forward.'

I remember this experience well. Naomi's story is very similar to mine. A few years into my own career break, I realised that looking after my children full-time was not what I wanted in the longer term. I knew that I wanted to go back to work, but it needed to be something I genuinely enjoyed, and it needed to be flexible. I spent many hours dreaming and chatting with friends about what this might be. One month, a friend and I got excited about importing baby equipment from Australia . . ., then a few months later I was inspired to set up a family focused travel agency . . ., then it was a flexible childcare business . . ., then studying psychology. I was never short of ideas. But the more options I thought of, and the more I talked about them and researched them on the Internet, the more problems I could see – and the further I got from actually doing them. Eventually, it got to the stage where I was reluctant to share my next great idea with my friends, because I had stopped believing that I was actually going to make any of them happen. Somehow, having too many choices was stopping me from pursuing any one option more seriously.

When I went on to study psychology, I found that this kind of decision paralysis is so common that it has a label: the 'paradox of choice' (see psychology box below). Put simply, too much choice in everyday life can make it difficult to choose at all. No choice is perfect, so we constantly have the feeling that there might be a better alternative – and we get stuck. The effect is inevitably stronger the more complex the choice is: a perfect storm when you're making career decisions.

Psychology: The paradox of choice

You might think that having many options makes it easy to find what you want, but the opposite is in fact true. Have you ever felt overwhelmed when standing in the cereal aisle or at the cheese counter at the supermarket, staring at all the options? Or standing in front of your too-full wardrobe, trying to decide what to wear? You're not the only one.

As the psychologist Barry Schwartz explains, 'with so many options to choose from, people find it difficult to choose at all'. And with so many options available we become overwhelmed from sifting through all the information available.

A classic research experiment – the Jam Study from 2000 – illustrates this phenomenon well. Psychologists Iyengar and Lepper set up two tables in a gourmet food store, at which shoppers were invited to taste and buy jam. One table, the 'extensive choice' table, had twenty-four varieties of jam; the other, the 'limited choice' table, had six. The study found that while more shoppers stopped at the twenty-four-jam table, people were far more likely to actually buy jam at the limited-choice table than the extensive-choice table (30 per cent versus 3 per cent).

The conclusion from the researchers was that the larger choice was overwhelming – in their words, 'demotivating'. Potential buyers hit 'choice overload', finding it just too hard to know which was best, so quite often they opted out of buying at all.

Naomi was sitting firmly in the paradox of choice. She didn't need any help with creating options – her challenge was how to narrow them down to a manageable number! It didn't take her long to create her decision criteria, as she'd already done so much introspection. She identified her top three strengths as relationship building, adaptability and analytical thinking. She had already built up a long list of her values, but she struggled to rank them. Eventually, she prioritised pure challenge (solving difficult problems), autonomy (high degree of control) and – she somewhat reluctantly admitted – status (senior job title) as her priorities. Her wide range of interests, from hiking to Asian art, had already led to several of her job options, but she was inclined to disregard her hobbies in the process – 'trying to follow my nose through my interests is what's got me into this mess!'

I explained to Naomi how to create a simple but powerful decision matrix spreadsheet to prioritise her options.

Self-coaching exercise: My decision matrix

1 List your decision criteria down one side of the paper.

2 List two to four of your previous jobs and the options you're considering across the top.

3 Work through the table job-by-job, ranking each job on each of your criteria according to whether it is a strong, medium or weak fit. If you don't know, put a question mark to flag that this is data you need to find. (Use the example that follows to help you if necessary.)

119

Decision matrix	Past job	Past job	New job	New job
Using strength of (add your strength, e.g. relationship building)				
Using strength of				
Using strength of				
Consistent with value of				
Consistent with value of				
Consistent with value of				
Some flexibility over				
Salary of at least				

Decision matrix – Naomi's example	Past job customer manager at bank	Past job wealth manager	New job copywriter for outdoors/fitness magazine	New job assistant at art gallery	New job HR role at bank	New job retrain as maths teacher
Using strength: relationship building	Strong	Strong	Weak	Medium	Strong	Medium?
Using strength: adaptability	Weak	Medium	Strong	Strong	?	Strong
Using strength: analytical thinking	Medium	Strong	?	?	Medium	Strong
Consistent with value: pure challenge	Strong	Strong	Medium	Medium	?	Strong
Consistent with value: autonomy	Weak	Weak	Strong	Weak	Weak	?
Consistent with value: status	Strong	Strong	Weak	Weak	Medium	?
Flexibility over core hours	Weak	Weak	Strong	Weak	?	Medium
Salary of at least [X]	Yes	Yes	No	No	Yes	Yes

Although Naomi was initially sceptical of how further analysis could help her ('Don't I just need to actually do something now?'), looking at how her past jobs rated on the matrix gave her confidence in the process. A role she had enjoyed earlier in her career received a high number of 'strong' ratings, even though she had been worn down by the aggressive company culture. She then scored the eighteen new options she was considering (see the subset below).

About a half of them – particularly those relating to her hobbies – were dominated by 'weak' ratings and so she was able to put them aside. For some of the remainder she realised that, despite her desk-based research, she knew very little about the reality of the role. She couldn't say, for example, if she'd be doing day-to-day activities she thrived on, or how much autonomy or flexibility she'd have. None of the options met all her criteria, but a handful had a promising number of strong or medium ratings.

Do what feels good

At this stage, I advise Naomi (and Jo and Mia) to choose three options to reality test against their decision criteria. I remind them that we're not dismissing the other options, just putting them to one side to allow for a focused exploration. Crucially, I ask them to choose their first set of options by doing what feels good to them, rather than proceeding more rationally. The question really is, 'What are you most excited to explore?' And try to put aside (for now, at least) the options which you think you 'should' do, or the options that you find yourself procrastinating about, thinking 'oh no, I have to do X now'. This should be an energising process!

If you're struggling to choose, here are two tips to help you follow your energy:

1. When you talk about each of your options, notice when your energy levels rise and when they drop. What are you most drawn to investigating? Talk to your friends and family about your options and see what they notice too.

2. Try describing yourself out loud, as if you're already doing each of your different options:

    - 'I'm running an Asian art gallery.'
    - 'I'm a wealth manager.'
    - 'I work for a top investment bank.'
    - 'I work for a boutique investment firm.'
    - 'I'm in charity fundraising.'
    - 'I'm a nutritionist.'

Which ones feel most like 'you'? Which would you feel most (and least) proud to say?

Jo found this exercise particularly useful: 'I hadn't realised I needed "permission" to step aside from the most rational or best paid options. I had been telling myself it was crazy to walk away from my TV career, after all I'd invested. Ironic, as there are so few jobs there now. But, once I gave myself more freedom, it was much easier to pick up on three jobs that actually made me feel energised and excited.'

Moving to action – test and learn

You've done a lot of thinking. Now it's time for some doing!

Crucially, you don't have to know the destination to take the first step in your return-to-work job search. In fact, delaying action because you're not yet sure of the ultimate destination is a big mistake. However, by 'take action' I don't mean jump straight into a big commitment! Even if you're really excited by one option, avoid rushing off to sign up for an expensive retraining programme or postgrad course, or immediately blasting out job applications.

The task at hand now is to reality test your shortlist of three. You need to fill the gaps in your knowledge, to find out 'what you don't know you don't know', and to test some of the assumptions you have made so far.

One example: say you're considering retraining into AI. You're fascinated by the topic, and there's a funded course on offer. You realise that you know what's involved in the training, but actually you're vague about the everyday reality of the opportunities open to you at the end. Or you're considering using your accounting skills in a public sector role, but you don't have any friends in the sector and you don't know how hard it would be to transition from private to public sector. Or similarly, you've worked in HR at big companies, and now you want to explore the same kind of role in much smaller companies. But you don't know how different the role might be when translated from a thousand people to fifty. This is the moment to look at your decision criteria spreadsheet and note down where your own question marks appear.

According to career transition expert Professor Herminia Ibarra in her book *Working Identity*, the best way to move towards a satisfying new career is to 'test and learn', as opposed to taking a traditional 'plan and implement' approach. She suggests that you:

Craft experiments Try out new activities in a small-scale way, like a fixed-term project, work shadowing or a temporary role.

Shift connections Make new contacts in the areas you are thinking about moving into, to find new role models and open up new opportunities.

With this 'test and learn' approach, you go out into the world and collect evidence to see if the jobs you're considering actually would be a good fit for you. What would you be doing day-to-day in the role? What is the culture of the organisation? Do you get on with the people working in this area? What we're talking about here is *active exploration* – getting out from behind your computer, speaking to people, 'trying before you buy'.

I've laid out below some of the best ways to gather the information you need.

Active exploration

Some ideas:

Informational interviews

The informational interview is not a new concept but, surprisingly, it's one that I find most returners don't consider. The idea is to use your networks to identify people doing the role, or working for the company or in the sector that appeals. You then ask if they would be happy to have a short conversation with you, purely to find out more about the job/company/sector. It's important to state clearly that you are not at the stage of looking for a job. Your aim is to gain information that you can't find online: such as the day-to-day reality of the job, the culture and working patterns of the company, growth areas and the types of roles available in the sector for people with your skills and experience.

To identify your interview targets, first consider whether there is anyone suitable within your circle of family, friends and local connections. Then ask your family and friends if they know of anyone suitable. For each person you speak to, ask them if they can put you in touch with anyone else who could help. Telling your story in a clear and credible way is important for this exercise to be effective, so do take a look at the next chapter before starting any interviews.

Attend free or low-cost events and conferences

You'll need to use your instincts to work out whether a sector or job feels like you. Immersion in the topic, in conferences or other events, is a great way to test this out. The aim is to put yourself in the middle of a large group of people who are already doing what you want to do. See if you're interested in what people are talking about – are you curious and wanting to learn more about the topics? Do they feel like like-minded people?

When I was considering retraining into occupational psychology, I attended a few conferences and came home buzzing with energy after the conversations I'd had and the talks I'd listened to. I was keen to talk to everyone about everything I'd learned. This made me feel so much more confident that this was a field I wanted to move into.

You might have the opposite experience, however. One returner

I knew was about to sign up for a degree in physiotherapy, as she'd become really interested during her break in the power of exercise and wanted to do something more rewarding. She attended a two-day physiotherapy conference and realised that, by the end of it, she felt more bored than anything. The topics covered were largely scientific rather than practical, and she acknowledged that it was the aspect of improving people's health that appealed to her, not the complex biology detail that she'd need to learn to retrain. As a result, she edited her must-have list to 'improving people's lives', added 'not overly scientific' to her must-not-have list, and redirected her efforts.

Work experience or shadowing

We tend to think that a 'work experience' day or week is just for teenagers, so it can feel embarrassing to even contemplate asking for work experience when returning to work. But if we accept that our aim, as we consider our career options, is to find out what people actually do day-to-day, observation is one of the best ways to achieve this.

You do need to be brave! One returner who had worked for an international events company wanted to find out the reality of working for a small firm. She knew the owner of a local events firm a little from the school gates, but it took her nearly a year to swallow her pride and ask if she could come in for a few mornings for some work experience, to help out with any tasks, however small. 'I must have almost dialled the number at least thirty times before I actually got the courage to do so! I was so afraid of sounding stupid.' She was happily surprised by the very positive response to her offer – the acquaintance suggested she come in the following week as they were busy and short-staffed. She found she loved the friendly and flexible team, and the work was much more interesting than she'd feared. Two months later she accepted a job there when a vacancy came up and she was still happily working there five years later.

Take a short course

If you're considering retraining through study, look for a short taster course first. When I was prevaricating about my options, I took an 'Introduction to Psychology' course in a local college. Being so fascinated by what I learned convinced me that going back to university was worth it. Conversely, another returner on my course found that the statistics side didn't appeal to her at all, and she was able to rule out retraining into psychology as a path that would suit her.

Skilled volunteering

You may well have taken on school, community or charity volunteer roles during your career break. This is a great way to make friends, feel productive and foster a sense of giving back. When you're ready to work, though, it is worth looking at volunteering more strategically. The aim with this is to seek out opportunities that might help you to brush up on your professional skills, refresh your experience, extend your network and, potentially, explore a new employer or area that you may be interested in working in.

As a side note, I'm very keen that returners should be fairly paid for their work, so I would only encourage working for free for a private-sector firm for a short period of time – effectively, as work experience. This issue – of striking the balance between 'getting back in' and 'knowing what you're worth' – can be especially thorny for returners, even at the point of a job offer. I will provide some advice on how to navigate this later on (Chapter 8).

A crucial piece of advice: make the time to explore

No one else can do this work for you. Meaningful exploration will only happen if you give it – and yourself – the time and attention you deserve. I know this can be difficult. You may have filled your life with activities that keep you busy, engaged and feeling productive. But you do need to carve out space for your return to work, and not leave it until you've done everything else that needs doing.

If there always seems to be something more important or time-consuming for you to do, consider why you don't feel able to make your career exploration a priority. We come back, now, to guilt.

What I hear from many returners – parents and carers in particular – is that it feels 'selfish' to be focusing on yourself. Remember (from Chapter 1): from a psychological perspective, feeling 'selfish' means you're telling yourself that you're lacking consideration for others and prioritising your interests above everyone else's. Usually, the opposite is in fact true, and this 'selfish' feeling is a by-product of having put your own needs to the bottom of the pile for so long. Try, then, to remember that balancing your needs alongside the needs of your family is not selfish. It's a healthy and positive attitude that is likely to improve your family life, as you will be happier and more energised.

Perhaps guilt isn't your problem. Perhaps you're just feeling ambivalent about whether you are ready to return – which means you procrastinate on this phase of career exploration to avoid having to move forward to the job search phase. Or perhaps it just feels scary to put yourself out there. You're perfectly happy doing research at your computer, but active exploration pushes you too far out of your comfort zone.

To help you over these barriers, take a look again at your 'why', to remind yourself of your motivations to return (on page 32). And have a re-read of Chapter 1, particularly on selfishness and ambivalence. Then start small: get your diary and block out twenty to thirty minutes, a few days a week, for career exploration. Do this for a month, ideally at a similar time each day. The regularity and repetition, plus the positive reinforcement of making progress, will help you to build your job exploration into a regular habit. Gradually, you can then expand the time you devote to it, as you move further into the job search stage. Some returners find it helpful to give their return-to-work activities a project name and to create an action plan for it, like any other work project. It's time to seriously focus on 'Project Me'!

How test and learn/active exploration looks in real life

Mia asked an old colleague, now in an in-house legal role, if she could come in for a couple of days to shadow him. She enjoyed her re-immersion in the legal world, but being back in a very structured corporate environment felt strangely restrictive for her. While talking to someone there, she heard about a different remote role with a public sector regulator that one of their friends was doing. This was one of the options that she'd highlighted in her job brainstorm, so she asked if she could be put in touch with the friend. When they started to talk about the day-to-day work in regulation, she realised that it ticked so many of her boxes. She would be doing much of what she enjoyed in her legal role, with the autonomy and flexibility that would enable her to actively manage her health.

Jo contacted a charity that was offering month-long work placements and decided to go for it when she was offered one. She came away from that month full of ideas and energy, and thinking about adjusting her pay expectations if she could find a role in a dynamic charity with a cause she believed in. She then got a place on a two-week 'Introduction to AI' boot camp and found it totally absorbing – she was excited to see how she could use her creative TV skills in a new way, and in an area that was expanding rapidly. From no options, she now had two she was seriously considering.

Naomi had narrowed down her long list to explore one previous role, in wealth management, and her five career change options down to two – a human resources role in a bank, and retraining as a maths teacher. She organised a day's work experience at a local school and quickly realised that, although the job would use many of her strengths, it didn't feel like her at all. Thriving with autonomy, she would feel too restricted by the confines of a strict timetable and syllabus. She then contacted a few ex-colleagues in banking and was able to set up some conversations with the wealth management team. Having catch-up conversations with her ex-colleagues did remind her how much she enjoyed the financial world. The more she discovered about wealth management, the better a fit it felt for her. The main stumbling block for her was the lack of flexibility, so she decided to focus her networking and research on investigating wealth management opportunities in organisations with a less bureaucratic, more flexible culture. She also found a friend of a friend in financial planning to chat to about both the training and the day-to-day job. She felt that this option could also tick her key boxes, but involved more exams than she'd expected – on this basis, she put it as her plan B.

Pulling it all together – intuition

Many of us, when we approach big decisions, tend to deliberately apply our rational, analytical skills and to distrust our more intuitive, emotional responses. We have been taught that 'gut feel' is misleading and will lead us down the wrong path.

Earlier, I asked you to put aside your more rational brain, and 'follow your energy' to decide which job options to research first. Now I am going to ask you again to de-prioritise your rational skills, but in a slightly different way: this time to tap into your intuition. If energy is the feeling of excitement that propels you towards an activity, then intuition is the calmer instinct that emerges when the other noise subsides.

Psychology studies have shown that for especially complex decisions, such as choosing a career, our rational faculties can easily become overloaded. In these situations, unconscious thought (our intuition) is an asset, not a hindrance.

If this feels surprising to you, consider the simple fact that whether we thrive in a job depends as much on how we feel about it as on how good it looks on paper. Our intuition isn't magic – but it is a super-fast response based on information in our long-term memory, developed through our lifetime of learning experiences. Our emotions are often linked to our underlying values. They can pick up something intangible (such as a company culture) that does or doesn't feel right before you can even explain the reason why.

I'm not suggesting that you jump right in at the start with a 'gut' reaction. Daniel Kahneman in *Thinking Fast and Slow* highlighted the many ways in which gut reactions can be false and trip us up. The point is that to make better decisions the aim is to consider your analytical responses alongside your less tangible, more intuitive responses.

Psychology: Intuitive decision-making

Have you ever found a solution to a problem you've been mulling over popping into your head while you're doing something else? Or knowing, when you list the rational pros and cons, that decision A looks best, but that you've a strong pull to go with decision B anyway?

This goes counter to the common belief that we always need to weigh up our options carefully before making a difficult decision. But it may well be that you're using your intuition, and to good purpose. Psychology studies compellingly show that intuition, or unconscious intelligence, can aid complex decision-making when deployed alongside more conscious, 'rational' thought. In simpler terms, deliberately thinking about something else can yield better results than consciously focusing on the decision.

Research by Dijksterhuis and colleagues (2004) illustrates this well. Participants were given detailed information about four different apartments, each with twelve attributes (for example, rent costs, location, size). They were told that the task was to decide which apartment was best. They were then either:

1   Asked to deliberate about the apartments for a few minutes (conscious thought), or
2   Distracted by a task to prevent conscious deliberation (unconscious thought), or
3   Asked to make an immediate decision.

The participants who made the best decision were group two: the people who were given the information and then were distracted, allowing their intuition to go to work. They chose the objectively best apartment more often than those in either the conscious thought or immediate decision conditions. Dijksterhuis repeated this finding in a real-life setting in 2006, finding that shoppers were more satisfied with significant purchases they made when decisions followed unconscious thought. He proposed the unconscious-thought theory to explain the apparent contradiction: first, that we can hold only a small amount of information in our consciousness, whereas the unconscious is much larger; second, that conscious thought focuses too much on the most plausible attributes, which are not always the most important to the decision-maker; finally, conscious thought follows set rules, so it is less able to cope in complex situations.

A study by Creswell and colleagues provided additional evidence that our minds continue to process information when we are distracted. They showed that the areas of the brain that are active while consciously considering a decision continue to be active in a period of distraction.

Therefore, alongside the reflection and analysis you've done (your self-snapshot, your decision criteria, your career research), don't ignore the extra evidence from your intuitive responses. Allow your feelings to play a significant part in your decision-making, alongside your rational pros and cons.

Active exploration is useful here in two ways. We've talked about how it helps to clarify whether the work you're considering meets your decision criteria (analytical). It is also one of the best ways to provide feedback to answer the crucial question: does this job feel like me? (intuitive). You cannot use your instincts from behind a computer!

How to tap into your intuition

If you find yourself deliberating too hard over your job options, take a break. Do something distracting that absorbs your attention for a few hours. This gives your unconscious mind the chance to work through the information, towards a decision. Then write down whichever decision you feel most drawn towards, before putting any more conscious thought into it.

A final thought

Career decision-making is not a one-off. The decisions you make now about your plan A and plan B are not fixed and final. As you get further into the job search process, you may find out new information – or you may uncover an exciting new option – that takes you into a different direction. For now, the aim is to keep moving forward towards a few work options that seem a great fit for you.

Active exploration isn't just useful for reality testing your ideas. It also helps to rebuild your professional identity (coming up in Chapter 6) and work networks (more on this in Chapter 7).

Summary

- It can be tricky to decide what to do next. You might have too few ideas, too many ideas, or you might know what you want to do but not be able to see how to make it work.
- Too much choice can stop you choosing anything at all (the paradox of choice), so you need to find a way to narrow your options down.
- Be creative about how you generate career ideas, and do involve other people.
- Once you have a shortlist of good options, dive in and reality test with an active exploration phase! Don't let uncertainty about the destination get in the way of starting the journey.
- Value your intuition and feelings alongside more rational pros and cons in making your job decisions.

'Go out and try new things! Reach out – people are happy to help. Keep exploring. It can lead you down paths that you never expected. Along the way you'll build your confidence and, most importantly, get clearer on what you'll enjoy and how you want to live your life now.' Naomi, now back at work as a wealth manager, after a ten-year break

6

'How do I talk about myself and my career break?'

How to Embrace Self-Marketing

B y now you will have been getting out and about meeting new people: attending events, taking courses, perhaps even applying for jobs. You're probably talking about yourself more than you've done in years, both in writing and in person. It's time to think about whether you're putting yourself across in the best possible way. Are you happy that you're telling your personal and professional story as clearly and confidently as you can? If not, this is the chapter for you.

'What do *you* do?'

Many people on a career break have learned to dread being asked the seemingly innocuous social introduction, 'What do *you* do?' They are not sure whether to talk about what they're doing now or what they used to do, all those years ago. The reply doesn't get any easier when you're planning to go back to work, when you also have to think about whether to mention what you want to do next (particularly if you're not quite sure yet). It's easy to flounder, underplay your experience or over-explain your break.

Consider Sara's reply: 'I've just been a stay-at-home mum for the last ten years. I know I haven't been using my education, but my younger son had some health problems as a baby and I wanted to be there for him. My previous job was very stressful and demanding, so I didn't feel that I could do both. I only planned to take two years off, but then we moved a few times and I had to settle the family in. And somehow a decade has flown past.' Sara used to stop there. Now that she's in job search mode, she sometimes adds, 'Now my children are older, I want to get back to work.'

Or Taylor: 'I was looking after my parents for a long time, as my father had dementia and then my mother had a stroke. I've done a few odd jobs along the way. My parents have both now passed away and I'm looking at options to get back to what I did before.'

Or Gita: 'I've not been working for a couple of years, as I've had very bad long COVID – some days I could barely get out of bed, and I felt short of breath almost all the time. I decided to leave my old work because I wasn't recovering and didn't feel I was doing my job as well as I needed to. Now I'm feeling stronger again, I'm thinking about a career change.'

All these returners have defaulted to explaining their current situation, only mentioning their old career in general terms. Their professional self is getting lost.

Why is it so hard to tell your return-to-work story?

When you're putting together your narrative, you have to make sense of the multiple identity shifts you've gone through, from the time you took your career break until now, together with the identity you're currently putting into play in trying to return to work. This narrative is even harder if the reasons for your career break are complicated or emotional with a lot to work through all in one go.

> 'In the last eight years I've been a carer for my parents, I've been in and out of hospital myself after a car accident, I've worked in a local shop, I've volunteered for a community befriending service, I set up a photography business from home. Now I want to get back into project management, should I mention all of this or none of it?' Taylor

Our identity is tied up with our actions – with what we actually do. A lot of people feel like a fraud if they try to claim back a previous (now distant, blurry) professional identity, when they have not done the job for so long.

> 'I don't know whether to say I'm a lawyer or an ex-lawyer, or whether to mention anything about being a lawyer at all. At the moment, most of the time I'm not even Sara, I'm just Gemma

139

and Arlo's mum. I haven't worked in law for ten years. I feel ridiculous saying now that that's what I used to do.' Sara

Talking about your career break can evoke strong emotions. Perhaps you feel deep down that you 'shouldn't' have stepped out of your hard-won career, and that you've wasted your qualifications and training. You might feel ashamed, embarrassed, as if you've somehow let yourself down. Perhaps you're full of regret. This in turn can make you defensive or apologetic about your career break.

> 'It was so difficult to get into medicine, and my parents were so proud of me when I qualified. I beat myself up for not using my qualifications. I don't enjoy telling people that I used to be a doctor, because they always ask me why I left such a perfect job. I'm embarrassed that I couldn't make it work through my illness. Now I feel I'll be even more judged for wanting to do something different.' Gita

Add to all this the fact that in many cultures we're brought up to be self-deprecating, to value humility and modesty. This is even more common if you're a woman, like the majority of career returners.

> 'I absolutely hate blowing my own trumpet. It feels so forced and uncomfortable.' Sara

Clearly, telling your return-to-work story can bring up a complex cocktail of thoughts and emotions. No wonder it's a lot to unpack in a few sentences to a new acquaintance.

Self-marketing – what it is (and isn't)

Telling your story is the core of your professional self-marketing: crafting and communicating the best possible version of yourself in a work context. Don't think of it as a negative thing. It's not about a fake veneer, 'style over substance' self-promotion, or pretending to be something you're not. With effective self-marketing, you're putting forward substantive information about yourself, about your skills, experience, values, attitudes and ambitions.

The skill is in the selection of what to include, the tailoring of the message and the emphasis you put on each aspect of your life. Aim to show the best and most interesting parts of yourself, focusing on those aspects which are most relevant to the person you're talking to.

Reframe: focus on what you can bring rather than what you can't

If telling our stories is inevitably a bit emotional, before you get going on crafting yours, I would like to encourage you to harness a positive emotion: pride. Don't hide your career break, own it! Don't think so much about what you lack or have missed, but shift your perspective, and the messages you give out, on to what positively differentiates you from a fresh graduate. Value the wealth of work and life skills, and experience, you have amassed before and during your break, together with the maturity and sense of perspective you bring.

In the same vein, I don't recommend burying your career break behind a skills-based CV/résumé, or hiding your age by including

141

only your last few jobs. This approach isn't sustainable when you get to interview stage, it creates ambiguity and – most importantly – it hugely downgrades your achievements and experiences.

Let's go ahead and make a strong 'business case' for you!

The career break sandwich

Back to the question: 'What do *you* do?' or 'Tell me about yourself.' Now, let's get practical.

I've developed a simple but effective structure to answer these questions, which has helped thousands of returners to create an engaging and credible professional introduction. I call it the 'career break sandwich', as your career break is neatly sandwiched in the middle of your story. The structure is in three parts:

1. Your background.
2. Your career break.
3. What you want to do now.

The career break sandwich allows you to put across the highlights of your professional credibility, to acknowledge – but not overly focus on – the important role that your career break has played in your life, and to situate yourself as purposefully moving back into a career. I don't want you to be vague, but nor do I want you to tell your full life story blow by blow.

This structure prioritises what we most want the listener or reader to remember, by harnessing the power of the primacy and recency effects: simply put, people are more likely to focus on, and remember, the first and last pieces of information you present them with. Therefore, on listening to your career break sandwich story, a person should walk away thinking: *This person has all this fantastic experience [primacy], and now they want to do this interesting thing [recency].* And then later on, these are the highlights that will have stuck with them.

Psychology: Primacy and recency effects

Read the following lists of character traits, and think about how you feel about the person being described:

Person 1: intelligent, industrious, impulsive, stubborn, envious.

Person 2: envious, stubborn, impulsive, industrious, intelligent.

Did you feel more positively about person 1? Many people do. But what you may not yet have noticed is that the traits in each list are exactly the same – just the order of the traits is reversed from person 1 to person 2.

Back in 1946, Solomon Eliot Asch, a pioneer of social psychology, posed this question to a group of research participants. He found that the people who read the list for person 1 felt pretty positively about the subject of the list, describing them as 'an able person with shortcomings'. The participants who read the list for person 2 felt much more negatively, describing the person as 'a problem, whose abilities are hampered by serious difficulties'.

Asch used this result to illustrate the 'primacy effect': a

mental shortcut whereby we pay more attention to the first pieces of information we come across. This is a common cognitive bias, one we experience frequently, day to day, every time we try to remember items on a list and find that the first items are the easiest to remember.

The primacy effect has a counterpart: the 'recency effect'. In a seminal 1966 study, Glanzer and Cunitz used a similar methodology to test people on their ability to remember words on a long list. Their study found that alongside remembering the items at the start of a list, people tend to remember the last few items at the end. It's the items in the middle that we forget. They proposed that this cognitive bias is because the recent items are still present in our short-term memory, so we can pull them out again easily (as long as there is not too long a delay).

Self-coaching exercise: My career break sandwich

1 Start with your professional background Summarise your work experience in one sentence, giving your years and field(s) of experience. For example, 'I worked for fifteen years in a variety of commercial roles in the consumer goods sector.'

Pick out the highlights of your working life and make these the career headlines in your story. Include key companies and clients you worked for or with, as well as a few relevant projects/ achievements ('In my last role, I was a global marketing manager for a leading consumer goods company and introduced one of their bestselling brands into Eastern Europe'). Do name any well-known brand companies and include any relevant professional qualifications, however old: an engineering degree or an MBA from twenty or thirty years ago still boosts your credibility today. Critically, don't minimise your achievements. This is the time to blow your own trumpet! In the same vein, avoid putting your successes down to luck or serendipity. Don't downplay your strengths, talent and hard work.

My background

2 Sandwich your career break in the middle This is the moment to confidently own your career break – don't apologise for it or justify it. Explain clearly and concisely why you've taken time out of the workplace. For example 'I took a career break to care for my young family and manage a relocation,' or 'I took a career break to look after my partner who had a terminal illness.' If you've had a painful reason for your break that you don't want to name, that's fine too: 'I took a career break due to a mix of challenging personal circumstances' can cover a variety of situations, and it signals that you don't want to discuss it in more detail. You can add more detail if you want. This is essential if you are pivoting your career because of a career break experience – such as moving into the education sector after enjoying related voluntary work. If you've had a variety of experiences, pick out the highlights that are most relevant in terms of skills development: study, voluntary work, entrepreneurial activity. Finally, include a few wildcards: anything unusual, such as time spent travelling or living abroad ('I've lived in four countries in eight years'), exploring different interests ('I did a masters in Chinese art') or doing something challenging ('I've started rowing competitively').

My career break

3 Finish with what you're looking for now, and why Summarise the type of opportunity you're aiming for and briefly explain why. Strike a balance between being too specific and too general ('Now I'm exploring using my project management and managerial skills in the education sector'). If you're exploring a few very different options, you can vary this section according to the context. And, whoever you're talking to, show or talk about your enthusiasm to be returning!

My career target

4 Craft it together into a credible and compelling story Now you have all the parts to your story, it's time to put them together into a narrative. Move away from pure chronology by pulling out key threads – this is how you make your story really compelling. Make links between your past, present and future. Have you always enjoyed helping people develop? Or solving difficult problems in a team? The aim is for these threads you pull out to weave seamlessly into what you want to do now.

Bring it all together

Once you have the essence of your career break story, it's time to develop various versions. Make sure you have ready your thirty-second introduction to a group of people you meet in a networking situation (this is what is known as your 'elevator pitch'). Then add a bit more colour to create a one-minute introduction that you can use in a more one-to-one situation, such as an informational interview.

Telling your story well takes a lot of practice. Try out your narrative first with family and friends. Get their feedback, ask them to tell you what is working as well as how you can improve. Telling and retelling allows you to rework your story until you feel comfortable and convincing. You'll know it's working well if your listener's follow-on comments or questions are about your future. You'll know you've totally cracked it if they offer helpful suggestions or start to talk about introducing you to other people who you should meet!

This is an outline of the story that Taylor developed:

'I worked in property development as a project manager for twenty years. When my father was diagnosed with dementia and then my mother had a stroke, I took a career break to look after them. Alongside full-time caring, I set up my own portrait photography business and enjoyed using my creative side. My parents both passed away last year and I considered scaling up my business. But I've missed my old career, so I'm looking at options to get back to project management, preferably in the construction sector.'

And Sara's draft:

'I'm a commercial lawyer and worked for a top international law firm for fifteen years. I really enjoyed the mix of the law and the business side. My last role was as a senior associate in the telecoms practice, managing a large international team. When my second baby had health issues, and we relocated to Japan and Bulgaria with my partner's job, I paused my career to focus on my family. Now my children are older, I'm excited to get back to work, and I am looking for a more flexible role as an in-house lawyer.'

And Gita's first version of her sandwich:

'I worked for eleven years as a doctor, training my way up to become a GP. Although the work was intense, I really enjoyed developing relationships with my patients. After developing long COVID in 2020, I ended up taking two years out to recover. I've had time to reassess what I want from the next stage of my career and I'm ready for a career change. I want to use my scientific skills in a new, more specialised way. I've become fascinated by tech and am considering retraining into cybersecurity.'

You can see here that the way you articulate your story is crucial. With the reworking based on the 'sandwich' structure, these are still Sara, Taylor and Gita's authentic stories, just told in a different way. There is a three-part benefit to this. One, to do with your confidence. If you reintegrate your old work life into your story, you immediately feel that you have more to offer an employer. Two, to do with your credibility. If you talk clearly about your skills, experience and break without mumbling or hesitating or repeating yourself, you're putting yourself across in the best way during networking, applications and interviews. Three, to enable people to help you. In networking conversations, if you explain your experience and what you're looking for, you're more likely to be told about relevant contacts or even job opportunities.

It is not by accident that I describe this core piece of self-marketing as a 'story'. We are wired in our brains to form and tell our own stories, to be curious about other people's stories, and to be fascinated by change (see psychology box below). Stories make information easier for us to remember. They simplify the complex, build empathy, and help us to make sense of the world, so do harness all that power when you talk about yourself! But you don't need to become an award-winning novelist to tell an effective story. Simply aim to pull out the most interesting information, talk about what's changed at this moment of your life – both practically and in terms of your personal evolution during your career break – and provide a clear structure, including an ultimate direction in terms of what you want to do next.

Psychology: The psychology of good stories

There have been many efforts (for example in Christopher Booker's *The Seven Basic Plots*) to decode stories, laying out the basic formats. The answer to the question 'What is a good story?' lies in the essential wiring of our brains, and how that wiring interacts with classic story recipes.

As Will Storr explains in *The Science of Storytelling*, 'Every story you'll ever hear amounts to "something changed". Change is endlessly fascinating to brains.' You can see this at work even in the simplest of children's stories. Something changes (the main character sets off on a journey; a parent dies; a plague falls across the land; someone comes into vast riches), and we are thrown into uncertainty. We want to know why and how things changed, and our brains are ignited to find out what will happen next.

This pre-wired curiosity suggests a natural, effective structure for telling your own story: (1) What's the status quo? (2) What's changed or is changing? (3) What are the challenges/uncertainties of changing? (4) What happens now? In essence: your career break sandwich!

Using your sandwich in other situations

Once you have the components of your career break sandwich assembled, you can adapt it for different contexts and different stages of your job search:

1 Use a shorter, more formal third-person version for your job application materials (CV/résumé profile). For example:

- Commercial lawyer for a leading international law firm [include name] for fifteen years, promoted to senior associate managing a large international team. After a parental career break, including relocations to Japan and Bulgaria, looking for an in-house commercial legal role.

150

2 Use a shorter, less formal first-person version for online professional social media profiles. For example:

- I worked as a commercial lawyer at [leading law firm] for fifteen years, managing a large international team. I took a break to look after my young children, including relocations to Japan and Bulgaria. I'm now ready to return to work and am looking for in-house legal opportunities.

3 When you make it to interview, create a longer version to reply to the inevitable, 'Tell me about yourself' question – this is the moment to add more details and build on the narrative thread. For example:

- I worked as a commercial lawyer at [leading law firm] for fifteen years, managing a large international team. Highlights included working on a big telecoms merger and speaking at an international industry conference. What I loved about that role was the pace and teamwork. When my second baby had health issues, and we relocated a few times, I paused my career to focus on family. Now my children are older, I want to get back to work. I'm looking for something that will use my management skills and challenge me in a research capacity, and I'm really drawn to the collaborative culture at your company.

4 Finally, in your early days back at work, you can adapt your sandwich to introduce yourself to new colleagues in a way that will make you feel credible and confident (for more on preparing for the early days back at work, see Chapter 9).

Hopefully, you can see how useful and crucial the career break sandwich can be. Despite their different backgrounds, experience and career breaks, Taylor, Sara and Gita all found huge power in crafting, owning and clearly articulating their return-to-work story. It helped them to make sense of their lives, to pick up the strands of their professional identity, and to feel the momentum towards the next chapter of their career.

Showing not telling

Self-marketing does not always need to be a narrative, though. It does not even always need to be something we speak out loud. If the career break sandwich works to tell people who we are and what we want, the rest of this chapter focuses more on how to *show* people these things.

Self-coaching exercise: Which three words?

Imagine someone meets you in an interview context. Afterwards, a colleague asks them what they thought about you. Which three words would you like them to use to describe you? Write these down. Make sure they are not bland or generic words, but specific enough to differentiate you. Test them out with a few people who know you well, to see if you can refine or improve them.

1

2

3

Once you're happy with these words as your 'business case', think about the following questions, to take your words into action.

Which parts of my story and CV really bring these words to the fore?

Which behaviours or traits of mine, related to these words, can I showcase in a networking chat or an interview, without me stating them out loud?

For Sara, trying to get back into law, the three words she came up with using the 'Which three words' exercise were: highly qualified, precise, approachable. She made sure to put her professional qualifications and team-management experience prominently on her CV (highly qualified), and had two friends proofread that and the 'master' draft of her cover letter (precise).

For Taylor, thinking about project management, the words were: creative, experienced, pragmatic. He knew that he wanted to talk in interviews about his photography entrepreneurial experience (creative) as well as his project management career (experienced), so he made sure to mention his photography business in response to the 'tell me about yourself' question.

Bear in mind here that the three words you choose might

not be exactly the same set for each application or interview. Sometimes you might want to focus more on your creative side, sometimes more on your analytical traits. Sometimes you might want to show your autonomy, sometimes how well you work with a team. You – especially as a returner – contain multitudes, have a wealth of experience, and part of the job here, just as with the career break sandwich, is in the judicious selection of detail.

Tailor your marketing

Which leads us to the next crucial piece of advice. When you get to the job search stage, you need to tailor the way you present yourself depending on who you're talking to, and what you're asking for.

It is not enough to put together a top-notch CV/résumé and cover letter, and fire off the same version of those to 100 companies (we'll talk more about the ins and outs and pitfalls of actual applications in the next chapter). Like any good marketing strategy, you should adjust your message, tone and mode of delivery between audiences. Which doesn't mean you should be a fundamentally different person from context to context. It just means that you should highlight different aspects of yourself according to the context and the reader or listener.

Here, it can be useful to consider self-marketing in two parts: I like the simple analogy of jigsaw pieces. Working out what you want to say or project about yourself is the first piece. The second piece is the role itself. Your task is to show, in written materials and face to face, how these two pieces fit together. That is, to demonstrate how (1) you are the best person for (2) this role and organisation.

Therefore, take all the information you've gathered about yourself (career compass, career break sandwich story, 'Which three words?', etc.) as raw material, and constantly be editing that material. You should decide for each role what goes in or comes out, what comes first, and how much detail to add. You should also make the link between the qualities you're drawing out about yourself and the detail of the role or organisation. You tell the international property firm looking for a senior manager more about how good you were at overseeing a large, diverse team, and tell the small charity looking for an operations manager more about how your values align with theirs. Here is where you have another edge over a fresh graduate: whereas they have a limited pool of information, you have the luxury of more choice!

In this way, you are simply doing some of the work for the recruiter. You're pointing out that you're a great fit for the role – and you're nudging yourself a step ahead by doing so.

First impressions matter

First impressions really do matter. People make assumptions very quickly about products, brands and people. I talked a little earlier about the primacy effect. There is an extension of this called the 'halo and horns effect' – in which our immediate impression of a person creates either a positive or negative lasting bias towards them (see psychology box below).

Psychology: Halo and horns effect

When you meet someone who is impeccably profession- ally dressed, do you assume that they'll be equally precise in their behaviours – reliable and dependable? Or do you find yourself assuming that someone who is warm and friendly on first approach is also likely to be generous and kind? If so, you might be experiencing the halo effect.

The halo effect was first described in 1920, in a study by psychologist Edward Thorndike. He asked army officers to assess their soldiers based on a series of attributes: some physical (for example, voice, physique, neatness) and some personal (such as intelligence, loyalty, cooperation). He found a clear cognitive bias in terms of assumptions about a relationship between the two kinds of attributes. In summary: if the officers' first impressions of a soldier's physical appearance were positive, this positively shaped their impressions of their other, unrelated, personal attrib- utes. Therefore, if a soldier was well-presented, with a strong voice and a powerful physique, they were assumed to be more loyal and intelligent, despite those personal qualities being as yet untested.

This illustrates a common positivity bias, the 'halo' of a positive first impression. This is reinforced by another mental shortcut, confirmation bias, whereby we tend to look for information that supports our existing views, and discount evidence which challenges it.

There is a vice versa to the halo effect: the horns effect. Just as positive first impressions tend to lead to further positive assumptions, negative first impressions often lead to further negative assumptions; for example, if we meet someone who is scruffily dressed, we might assume that they are less intelligent and are disorganised in their work.

The most researched trigger for both halo and horns is physical appearance, but other traits can play into these effects too. For example, if we encounter someone who is enthusiastic and friendly, we often assume that they are more than averagely competent – one to remember in interviews and networking conversations!

You can aim to create a halo (positive) effect by presenting yourself confidently and credibly from the outset, first in your applications and then in interview conversations.

Here is some halo advice that applies to any job seeker:

- Put your most relevant highlights front and centre.
- Avoid woolly, generic or unsupported statements.
- Get a friend to proofread your application material – it's easy to miss spelling and grammar mistakes.
- For online and face-to-face meetings, arrive a little early.
- Enter the (real or virtual) room looking confident and smiling, keeping eye contact and with uncrossed arms.
- Start a conversation with an enthusiastic tone and aim to radiate positive energy.
- And finish strong! Don't forget the recency effect that goes along with the primacy effect. End with a positive statement and a smile, and follow up with a positive thank you message.

Here's some halo advice, in particular as a returner:

- For online meetings or interviews, practise the tech in advance. There is an unfortunate assumption (see Chapter 7) that returners won't be tech-savvy. If you 'arrive' late to the interview, flustered, and saying something like, 'Sorry I'm not great with technology,' you reinforce the assumption that returners, and especially older applicants, won't be able to catch up with workplace tech advances.

- Don't just dig out your old work suit. Make sure that what you wear makes you feel professional and up-to-date, and that it reflects the image you want to create. (Again, we will cover appearance more in the next chapter.)

- Don't go straight in (on paper or in person) talking about flexible or part-time work – it might give the recruiter the impression that the job/company itself is less interesting to you than the working pattern. Prove that you're the right person first, get them sold on you, and then talk later (see Chapter 8) about negotiating your preferred ways of working.

- During the interview, draw attention to your strengths rather than pointing out your weaknesses. The push to 'be your authentic self' can lead to oversharing. My advice is to be yourself, but to be the best half of yourself! Focus on what you do bring, rather than what you don't.

Summary

- Returners often struggle to talk about themselves confidently and credibly: their confidence is low, their break has been complicated.
- Taking time to craft and practise your return-to-work story is crucial.
- Self-marketing does not mean style over substance or massaging the facts – it just means putting your best self forward.
- Own your career break! Don't apologise for it, justify it or hide it.
- Harness the power of primacy and recency, and the principles of good storytelling by crafting a career break sandwich that you can adapt for various situations.
- Consider which three words you would like to showcase about yourself in written materials and face to face, and what parts of your experience bring those alive.
- Always, always tailor your marketing.
- First impressions really do matter.

'Step back and view yourself as a brand: as a product you need to sell. Look on your career break in a positive way, and tell your story proudly. It's so empowering to talk about your many years of experience and achievements – to start to see your age as an asset, rather than a barrier.' Bettina, now back at work as a brand marketing manager, after a six-year break

7

'Why is my CV disappearing into a black hole?'

How to Find Your Return-to-Work Job

It may have been a while since you wrote a job application: for some years, even decades, if your early career was with only one or two employers. Or you may have fired off tens or hundreds of job applications before even picking up this book – and had little or no success, which is why you're reading this now. You might feel that you're doing all the right things, your self-marketing is robust, but you're still not getting anywhere. You're agonising about where you're going wrong. You feel stuck ... again.

Joao worked for over twenty years in risk management before, desperate for a change, he decided to go on an adventure with his partner. They moved to Indonesia and set up a small business doing house renovations. What was supposed to be a three-year break ended up being six years. He came back, now fifty years old, 're-energised' and raring to go. He started looking for work. Nine months later, he says, 'The recruitment agencies who used to chase me weren't interested at all when I got back in touch. And even though I have applied for many, many jobs, which I am more than qualified to do, I haven't been able to get even one interview. No one will give me any feedback, in fact, usually I don't even hear back – it's like sending my CV into a black hole. It looks like no employers are going to hire someone at my age with a gap like mine.' He is wondering whether to apply for much lower-level jobs to increase his likelihood of success.

Justine worked in operations at an investment fund, before taking a three-year break for mental health reasons. She says: 'Everyone tells me I'm most likely to find a job now through my network, so I've had endless coffees and lots of good conversations, but only one has resulted in a concrete job opportunity.' When I ask her what she wants to do she says, 'Something analytical, with more of a purpose than I had before.' She was really excited by one 'dream job' lead she finally got – a similar role to her last one, but in a small outfit focused on ethical investing. She put all her efforts into this, but after a painfully slow recruitment process, she got to the second-round interview stage before being rejected in favour of an internal candidate: 'I had my heart set on that one, and now I'm crushed, as I have to start all over again.'

Reality check: recruitment bias

'It looks as if no employers are going to hire someone with a gap like mine, particularly at my age . . .' The frustrating reality is that your career break is a barrier in traditional recruitment. You're not imagining things. Too many recruiters arc biased against candidates with a CV/résumé gap.

It is tough enough to get a job in a (frequently very competitive) open market – no matter where you live or what sector you work in or what stage of your career you're at. Recruiters and hiring managers are frantically busy, often receiving hundreds of applications for each job they advertise. They typically feel overstretched and under pressure, with too many roles to fill in too little time. They become risk averse – they want to find a candidate who can quickly fit into the team and 'hit the ground running'. As they churn through applications, it's easy for them to make assumptions – unconscious or conscious – about whether you will 'slot right in'. They make rapid-fire screening decisions based on certain details that jump out at them, starting with your current role (or the lack of one).

This is when the lazy stereotypes about career returners kick in. I call it the 'triple-whammy' of bias:

1. There is a widespread recruiter bias against CV gaps, due to a false perception that skills deteriorate when people take time out of their career. (A Harvard Business School Study in 2021 in the USA, Germany and the UK found that 44 per cent of automated hiring systems filter out middle-skills candidates with employment gaps of over six months in their CV/résumé.)
2. If you have been a full-time caregiver or have taken a low-level job to fit in with family life, you hit other biases too. You can be seen as a 'homemaker', with an implied assumption that you will be less ambitious, less flexible and will prioritise family over work. From my own experience,

this is also evidenced by the fact that even enlightened employers often assume that all returners with children will only want to work part-time. (Weisshaar's 2021 study found that 'positive information on past job performance and social skills eliminated hiring disadvantages faced by unemployed job applicants, but non-employed caregiver applicants remained disadvantaged, suggesting more entrenched bias.')

3. Finally, if you are older than forty-five – as many returners are – you may also encounter age-related bias, which increases as you head towards and into your sixties. You'll have to counter the stereotypes that, as an older worker, you'll be scared of technology, that you'll struggle to learn new skills, and that you won't keep up with the pace of the modern workplace. (Lössbroek's 2021 vignette survey across managers in nine European countries found that older candidates, particularly those over fifty-five, consistently received lower hireability scores.)

Counter the bias

I've laid out the depressing biases. Rest assured that there are many people – myself included – working with employers and govern-ments who try to tackle these on a macro level. We're making progress, but societal change takes a long time, so you need to take action yourself, rather than waiting for the world to change.

The good news is that there are many thousands, even millions, of people around the world back at work after very long breaks. How have they managed it?

First of all, not all employers hold these biases (see below). Second, you can counter the biases. Refuse to feed into them, provide evidence that you don't fit the stereotype, and look for creative ways to reduce your perceived risk to employers. You can do this with your self-marketing and how you present yourself (see Chapter 6). You can also do it with who you approach, and how you approach them.

Before we start: the mindset with which you approach the recruitment process can be the difference between persevering and giving up. Don't be easily defeated! Aim to be 'realistically optimistic' (more on this later). A series of knockbacks might have you convinced that no employer will ever want you, but try not to generalise your bad experiences to assume that *all* your experiences will be the same. There are metaphors you can use to help here, to create an image of possibility, so think of the biases not as roadblocks or insurmountable barriers, but as hurdles that you can jump over with a bit of practice and effort.

To look back to Chapter 3 for a moment, I urge you to choose to believe that although getting back to work might not be easy, it is definitely achievable.

Some good news before we get going on practicalities: ever-increasing numbers of employers recognise the skills, experience and perspective that returners can bring to their organisations. They are out there looking for you! Take a look at the Career Returners website to see all the programmes and events that are going on. As one successful UK returner put it:

'We are lucky to be living at a time when there are a growing number of organisations who are focused on supporting and mentoring you to get back on the career ladder and are actually rooting for your success.' Daniel, copywriter, after an eight-year break

Read these quotes from real-life employers to give yourself a boost.

1 Employers see you as great talent:

- 'We hire returners because it makes business sense, not just because it is the right thing to do. We need returners!'
- 'It's a key part of our talent strategy; as a customer-obsessed company we want to represent the diversity of the community in which we operate.'
- 'Finding experienced talent is always challenging, even for larger firms – returners offer a pipeline of new talent which we are really happy to invest in.'

2 They value you because you bring something different:

- 'If you have a truly inclusive strategy, you value people from all backgrounds and experiences.'
- 'Returners are really highly valued throughout the business. They are valued for the experience they have – they bring something different to the table.'
- 'Returners offer unique skills and experience.'

3 They appreciate the skills and attitudes you bring:

- 'Returners bring a lot of determination and motivation to their roles. They have that extra oomph that they really want to prove themselves, and they bring a fresh perspective that is really valued.'
- 'Their talents have increased with their break in terms of learning other skills such as perseverance, communication, and flexibility.'
- 'Returners are highly capable, highly talented and uniquely brave, because they're taking themselves out of their comfort zone to return to work after an extended career break.'

Job search principles

With this positive boost to your mindset, now let's dive into the practicalities. There are many universal job search skills – such as CV/résumé writing and interview skills – which we won't go too deeply into here. They are covered in myriad books and online advice, and are often role, sector or country specific. What I want to give you instead are fundamental routes, tactics and attitudes for applying for a job after a career break.

Joao's job search plan was typical of many returners: firing out multiple applications via online job adverts and recruitment agencies. When you're at the active job search stage, it's tempting to set yourself a target of applying for a certain number of jobs a week, hoping to maximise your chance of hitting the bullseye. But, as Joao found, this scattergun approach rarely works, and particularly not as a returner. If you're applying for hundreds of jobs, you're most likely not tailoring your applications for each role. Or even applying for the right things.

Narrowing down your options too much, like Justine, to the one perfect 'dream job' isn't going to help you either. You put all your eggs in one basket and, if you get rejected, you feel as if you're back to square one. This is terribly dispiriting and is likely to painfully prolong the process.

How to target routes back to work

I urge you to think outside the 'open market' box in how and where you look for roles. The key is to be targeted and creative. Give plan A your best shot, but appreciate that even if you do all you can, you might just be in the wrong place at the wrong time. Actively pursue a plan B and a plan C at the same time. And don't rule out options that aren't perfect. Stepping-stone roles can be a good route back if you've had a very long break, if there's very little hiring going on in your sector, or if you are aiming for a career pivot. Remember: the road to a job you love might be winding, and it may take a few steps, but believe that you will get there.

These are some 'targeted and creative' options which I consistently see working well for career returners – I'll explore them in more detail below:

1. Look for returner programmes and other returner-friendly employers.
2. Look for opportunities with a built-in trial period.
3. Use your networks.
4. Consider freelance work.
5. Consider stepping-stone skilled volunteering.

Look for returner programmes and other returner-friendly employers

Many leading employers have started targeting career returners through specialised returner programmes. These are supportive employment programmes specifically designed for candidates who have taken long career breaks (the criterion is usually a career break of at least eighteen months, but sometimes one or two years). Returner programmes are most common in the UK, USA and India, but there are initiatives springing up around the world. Although the majority of programmes have been in financial services and STEM multinational firms, there is an increasing spread across private and public sectors, with some smaller firms also seeing the benefit of targeting a well-qualified and relatively untapped talent pool.

You can find these programmes advertised on company websites and through specialised returner organisations such as the one I co-founded, Career Returners. They may run annually, or a few times a year, with a small peer group of returners starting together. Or they may run on a rolling basis with people joining one-by-one into available roles. There are a few different types of returner programmes, so I'll talk them through for you.

Many of the programmes are known as 'returnships'. With a returnship, you take on a professional placement, leveraging your skills and experience. You'll be doing real work, in a similar role to the one you left or using your transferable skills in a career pivot job (same role, different sector; same sector, different role). Returnships are paid and usually last three to six months. There is the likelihood of a permanent role at the end if the programme is successful for both sides – although this is not guaranteed. Support is provided through the transition period in terms of training, mentoring and/or coaching.

Returnships have a built-in trial period for both returner and employer. This lowers one of the biggest return-to-work barriers – the perceived risk for the employer – and it also enables you to try out whether the employer and job are a good fit for you. The downside is that you have to cope with the uncertainty of not knowing for sure if there will be a permanent job at the end, and to make sure that you make the most of the placement in any event. However, the odds are good – with many well-planned returnships 80 per cent or more returners are offered ongoing roles at the end of the placement.

Another returner-focused route back to work is known as a 'supported hiring' (a term I coined in 2015) or 'direct returner hire'.

In this case, you start directly into a permanent role, rather than a placement, so there is less uncertainty. This stability could be a huge factor if you're returning for financial reasons in particular. Some employers run supported hiring as a programme once or twice a year for small groups. Other employers advertise ad-hoc 'returner roles' which they feel would suit a returning professional, and a small number welcome returner applications for all their open roles. With supported hiring, you are likely to have a similar wrapper of transition support (training, mentoring and/or coaching), but this support might not be as comprehensive as on a returnship and you may not start with a cohort.

If you can find a returner programme or a returner role in your country and sector, this could be exactly what you're looking for: a supportive bridge back to a suitable-level role. Many thousands of people returning after long breaks have successfully resumed their careers through this route.

'Initially when I started to look for a new role, I really struggled. I didn't get any responses at all. I assume it was due to my fifteen-year break. Then one of my friends told me about returnships. I signed up with Career Returners and within two months I got on a returnship. Initially I was scared, but the support I've received has made my journey smoother and I have now secured a permanent position.' Diana, insurance underwriter, after a fifteen-year break

'Prior to getting on a returner programme, I got quite dispirited at never being asked for an interview due to my career break and my lack of local experience, despite my skills being strong. The programme has offered me the flexibility and support I needed and has proved to be a soft landing into a great job.' Ike, mechanical engineer, after a two-year break

If you're interested in a career change, there are also some returner retraining programmes, into areas such as software development and financial planning. These are paid career change programmes combining training (upfront and/or on the job) with work experience to build you towards a new qualification. They may be standalone programmes for returners, or existing programmes for mid-career switchers or early graduates which now also target returners. The plus is that you could have the opportunity to restart in a new field with exciting development potential, without paying for expensive training yourself.

You're likely to be starting in a more junior role, however, so you'll need to be ready to work your way up again.

'After my career break, I really wanted a change and a new challenge. I was excited to be accepted on to a financial planning retraining programme. I enjoyed the workout that the exams gave my brain. Working hard for exams was great for my children to see – they were nagging me to revise rather than the other way around! I have learnt so much.' Lucille, financial planner (retrained), after an eleven-year break

A note of caution: don't make returner programmes your sole strategy. They can be a fantastic opportunity, but they are not a silver bullet. The programmes can be very competitive – they do not yet exist in great numbers and are only in some sectors and countries. I would urge you to also use some of the other strategies outlined here to find an opportunity that fits with your skills, values and motivations.

Look for other returner-friendly employers

How can you identify employers who are likely to be open-minded about candidates with career breaks, even if they're not saying it upfront in their advert?

1. Look carefully at corporate websites and social media. Is the employer taking tangible action to attract and support different types of candidates for their roles, such as people who are neurodiverse or army veterans?
2. Look for employers advertising on job boards and with recruitment agencies that are targeted at a demographic you fit into: women, parents, carers, ethnic minorities.
3. Look beyond the brand-name employers to smaller and local firms. Employers who are less well known, and receive fewer applicants per role, often recognise the need to access new talent pools.
4. Look for sectors with skills shortages. Employers struggling to fill their roles are often more welcoming towards candidates with non-linear career paths.

If, in the course of your research, you've narrowed down the employers you're keen on to a few targets, but you can't see any advertised opportunities, you could try a direct approach in case there are any suitable roles in the pipeline. This can work especially well with smaller firms, as it's easier to reach a decision maker. If you're interested in larger companies, this is most likely to succeed if someone in your network can introduce you. The key is to carefully research the company and identify who best to approach, then to use your career break sandwich story (page 142) to succinctly explain your strong interest in the organisation, and what you can bring.

Look for opportunities with a built-in trial period

Another angle is to look for short-term job opportunities that help you get your foot in the door of an organisation. Examples are maternity/paternity, sabbatical or long-term sickness covers. These are a good route to target, as they work along the same psychological lines as a returnship for a hiring manager. There is a built-in trial period, so the manager is often less worried about 'taking a risk on a returner' (their words, not mine!). Also, importantly, short-term roles are much harder to fill than permanent roles, so you'll face less internal and external competition.

Interim or contracting roles are another option. These tend to work better for returners who have had shorter breaks or who have recently reskilled, as there's likely to be more pressure to immediately deliver. They can however feel less committing than a permanent role, and give the opportunity to take time out between contracts, which may suit your circumstances.

'After two years away from work, with multiple family bereavements and my own health issues, I decided to rejoin the marketing world slowly by taking on short-term contracts and interim roles, taking breaks in between roles. This helped me to get ready to take on a full-time role again.' Louise, marketing director, after a two-year break

Offering to work on a specific project can be another great introduction to an organisation. Organisations rarely advertise project work, so this is most likely to come via your networking contacts.

All these short-term opportunities give you a chance to impress an employer and may lead to a permanent role. Even if they don't, see them as a springboard to another role. Even short-term work will have refreshed your skills and experience, and helped to rebuild your confidence and professional networks.

Use your networks

I've already talked about networking, in Chapter 5, as a way to gain career insights and ideas. Your networks are also, without doubt, one of the most reliable ways to get back into a job. From my own observation, a high percentage of returners secure their first role back through a job offer from an ex-colleague, a recommendation from a friend or a serendipitous conversation at a social event.

Why is networking such a powerful tool when you're finding your path back to work? Once again, it's all about risk reduction. Imagine that a particular hiring manager is risk averse and carrying around some of the stereotypical biases towards returners that I talked about earlier. Now, imagine you used to work with this person, or someone in their own organisation has vouched for you, or that you have met and impressed them in a personal context. The effect of this network link is to blow through the bias against returners. You are far more likely to get a positive halo effect (described on page 156) instead!

The strongest effect is, unsurprisingly, when you approach a manager you've worked with in the past. As they remember exactly how capable you were in a professional role – whether that was two or twenty years ago – your career break fades into insignificance. In fact, to anyone you used to work with (as a team member, direct report, client or supplier) you are the same professional person you were back when they knew you. Many returners find, once they call their ex-colleagues to say that they're ready to return, they're back in a job before they know it.

There are other benefits to getting out and about talking to people. Crucially, networking puts you in the right place to hear about the 'hidden job market' – opportunities which aren't being posted publicly, but rely on word-of-mouth marketing, or jobs which are still in the pipeline.

The power of networking is good news for returners! If you don't believe this, and you are thinking that you've lost your networks, have a go at the 'My network grid' exercise below. Mapping out your network is much easier than it used to be, as professional social networks are great for helping you to identify and reconnect with old contacts. You may be surprised by the breadth and depth of the network you've built up during your life. This set of contacts is another key advantage you have over a fresh young graduate.

Self-coaching exercise: My network grid

1   Draw up a grid with the areas of your life at the top.

2   Under each heading, write down the names of all the people you can think of that you could speak to, whether you last saw them yesterday or ten years ago.

3   Have a look at your list and underline the people you feel most comfortable talking to.

4   Now star anyone you think could be helpful in your job search: they could be working in an area of interest to you (or related to someone who is) or they could simply be well-connected, so they would be likely to have friends of friends who could help.

5   The people you have starred and underlined are your priority contacts. These are the people to approach first to tell them that you're actively job seeking. As you get more confident, work through the list.

6   Look for opportunities to build your network – for example, by going to a professional association, alumni group or local community event.

School	Further education	Work	Family	Friends/ community	Sport/ hobbies	Other

To harness the power of your network, you'll have to overcome any reluctance about using it. I have found that returners often don't mind networking at the exploration stage but feel awkward further down the line when it comes to saying that they're looking for a job. However, holding back only hurts your chances of success.

You do need to tell people that you're actively job seeking, and give them a good idea of what type of role and/or sector you're interested in, so that they will be able to help you. Ex-colleagues may be most directly connected to potential employers, but don't miss out on telling friends, family and wider acquaintances too. Often a pivotal introduction or a recruitment lead comes from a surprising source.

Here are some examples to illustrate how networking can be incredibly helpful at the job search stage:

Maria used to work in a programme management role, then took a career break to look after her two young children. Five years later, keen to get back to work, she reached out to a few people she had worked with in the past, explaining that she was looking for a role where she could use her sales and project management skills. 'I wasn't at all confident that I'd have any luck, but reaching out to past contacts turned out to be the best thing I could have done. My now-manager replied, and I ended up back at work at a tech company within three months. As I knew him from before, there was the benefit of knowing he'd be a supportive boss.'

Sam said, 'I assumed that my old career was closed to me after ten years out. I got nowhere with applying for jobs I saw advertised, even those I was well qualified to do. It took me ages to get in touch with old colleagues. I felt embarrassed to say that I hadn't worked as an engineer for so long and was looking to get back. But eventually I did just that and got two interviews leading to job offers within a week, one from a friend of a friend and one from contacting my ex-manager to say I was looking to return. My skills were just waiting to be used again.'

Bhindi told a new acquaintance at a social event that she was a chartered accountant looking for a three-day-a-week business finance job, to work around caring for her mother. The contact put her in touch with a friend who had recently said he was struggling to find part-time strategic-finance support for his small business. They met, immediately connected, and she started the job the next month. This is a perfect example of creating your own luck (more on this later). She advises other returners, 'Make yourself visible. Tell people what you're looking for or they won't think to tell you when they hear about opportunities.'

You never know where your 'lucky break' might come from!

Consider freelance work

Self-employment, in terms of setting up your own business, isn't a core focus of this book. However self-employment as a free-lancer – that is, offering your skills to companies or individuals on a project-by-project basis – is important here, because it's a common route back to work for returners. Be very clear, before you jump in, on what specific skills you want to offer and your USC (unique strengths combination) (Chapters 2 and 4 can help with this).

The upside of freelance work is the high degree of control over where, when and how you work. This can be a huge benefit if you enjoy autonomy and are looking to work very flexibly around your children or caring responsibilities, or to manage your workload for health reasons. The downside is that you will have much less security than in an employed role, and you're likely to have peaks and troughs in your work and income.

If you're looking to find work directly, you will also need to feel comfortable with networking and 'selling yourself'. Approaching former work colleagues is the easiest place to start. Once you build a reputation, the selling side becomes easier. If you don't enjoy selling, you can look to tie in with one or more larger organisations, including virtual professional services and training businesses, who take on skilled professionals as 'associates' or 'consultants' to staff their projects.

Sandra had had a successful career in HR, and then four years of being a full-time parent. 'I was desperate to get back to work, but reluctant to head back into the corporate world. I met up with a good friend who told me about an organisation hiring freelance trainers/facilitators. The selection process was nerve-wracking, but I came through. I now work around two days a week, with a six-week summer break, delivering the courses to a wide range of businesses. A new career has opened up for me.'

Freelancing could be a short-term option – a stop-gap when your children are young or a way to refresh your skills and ease back into employed work. Or, if you find it suits you, it could become your longer-term way of working.

Consider stepping-stone skilled volunteering

In Chapter 5, I talked about volunteering in a role that uses your skills as a great way to refresh your experience, rebuild your professional confidence and networks, and, potentially, explore a new employer or area that you might be interested in working in. Skilled volunteering can also be a stepping stone into a great job.

If you're considering working for a charity, volunteering is not only the best way to test out whether not-for-profit life is for you, but it's also often the main route to a paid job.

For Susie, taking a role as a school governor was a perfect way to revive her people-management and influencing skills. 'I wasn't paid for the role, but in every other way it was a real job using all my skills, so my confidence came back quickly. It was great recent experience to talk about on my CV and at interview. The manager interviewing me for the project management role I eventually landed agreed that there's no harder leadership task than engaging a group of volunteers.'

Targeted volunteering can also be a more direct launchpad back to work. If you're planning a career switch into the not-for-profit sector, there is usually a clear-cut volunteer-to-staff pathway. For private sector roles in start-ups or smaller firms (although I'd caution you against offering your services for free for a lengthy period), carefully targeted volunteering might also lead you directly into a job.

Rana's successful return to work came through a combination of a targeted direct approach and strategic volunteering. Seven years after leaving her architecture job, she summoned up the courage to contact a local firm. 'My initial approach was based on a wish to gain some experience and rebuild my knowledge. I offered to support a few mornings a week on a volunteer basis.' She also saw this as a way to test out whether a local firm would offer the type of work she enjoyed. After six weeks, she was convinced that this was the right place for her and, impressed with her skills, the firm offered her a part-time role. 'I've now been in my role for two years and love it.'

Stop/start/continue: your coherent plan

I've covered a range of suggestions in this chapter so far. Some of these you may already be doing, others may be new ideas. Now is the moment to distil all this information into a coherent plan. The 'Stop/start/continue' coaching exercise can be helpful here.

Self-coaching exercise: Stop/start/continue

This simple exercise is great for helping you to develop a job search action plan, focusing your attention on the most productive activities.

1   Write down three job search activities that, when you reflect on them, are actually not very effective, or are taking too much time relative to their reward. These are the activities you will STOP doing.

2   Look at the targeted and creative strategies above as a prompt, and then write down three activities that you're not currently doing but now you'll START doing.

3   Write down three activities you're currently doing which you are finding helpful, and make a note to CONTINUE with these.

If you can't quite think of three activities in each section, or you can think of more in a particular section, that's fine. Aim for at least five start/continue actions.

Stop	Start	Continue

Stop/start/continue – Joao's example

Stop:

- Chasing recruitment agencies who don't want to talk to me.
- Applying a scattergun approach for any role I'm qualified for.

Start:

- Identifying returner-friendly employers: target their open roles (and returner programmes if relevant); look for a network contact; try a direct approach.
- Looking for short-term roles to get a foot in the door.
- Looking for skilled volunteer roles and work experience to refresh my skills.

Continue:

- Being optimistic, with positive expectations about the future.
- Getting out and about, renewing and making connections.
- Applying for advertised jobs - just in a focused way, no more than one a day.

For much of the remainder of this chapter, I'm going to move from practicalities to mindset. The right attitude to job seeking is just as important as sending out the right applications.

Focus on mindset, Part I: create your lucky break

Many returners talk about finding their job through 'luck'. But what does 'luck' in the context of finding a job really mean? It's not – like winning the lottery – pure chance, a flash of out-of-the-blue randomness. In a job search, luck means being in the right place at the right time, talking to the right person. And in most cases that 'luck' is not random, but comes from your own work and instincts and persistence. You create your own luck!

Psychology studies have found that the more creative, curious and open-minded you are, the more opportunities will arise. And the more you see yourself as 'lucky' and believe that good things will come, the more likely you are to spot the path towards those good things when it presents itself (see psychology box).

Psychology: The psychology of luck

Why do some people always seem to be in the right place at the right time? Psychologist Richard Wiseman spent eight years carrying out interviews and experiments with several hundred people, from the ages of eighteen to eighty-four, who saw themselves as exceptionally lucky or exceptionally unlucky. In 2004, he pulled together his findings on how luck can change our lives into a book, *The Luck Factor.*

In one striking study, he gave participants a newspaper and asked them to read through and say how many photos were inside. On average, 'unlucky' people took two minutes to count the photos. 'Lucky' people took seconds! The difference? There was a half-page message on page two that read: 'STOP COUNTING – THERE ARE 43 PHOTOS IN THIS NEWSPAPER'. The 'lucky' people saw it, stopped and responded. The 'unlucky' people missed the opportunity and continued counting.

This summed up the key finding from Wiseman's years of research into luck: to a large extent, people make their own luck, good and bad, by the way they approach life. He identified four behaviours that characterise 'lucky' people:

1   They create, notice and act upon chance opportunities (for example, they meet a large number of people day-to-day, so they have more opportunity to meet someone who will have a positive effect on their lives).
2   They trust their intuition and gut feelings when making decisions.
3   They have positive expectations about the future and attempt to achieve challenging goals.
4   They aren't immune to bad luck (it happens to us all), but they don't dwell on it, and they persevere through setbacks until their luck turns.

The great news is that Wiseman also found that luck is a skill that can be learned. In a Luck School, he trained 'unlucky' people to think and behave like 'lucky' people. After only four weeks, 80 per cent said their luck had increased, on average by over 40 per cent! To create your own luck, he advises taking it step by step, 'start by connecting with a few more people, listening to your inner voice just a little more, having slightly higher expectations about the future ... slowly but surely, you will become a luckier person'.

Focus on mindset, Part II: realistic optimism

We've talked in this chapter about creativity, open-mindedness and 'making your own luck'. In terms of attitude on the return-to-work journey, I often also refer to 'the 3Ps': positivity, patience and persistence. Now I'd like to introduce one more crucial mindset concept: realistic optimism.

Optimism sounds like a universally good thing, right? In fact, being too optimistic in your job search, without adding a dose of realism, can be unhelpful. You might underestimate the effort needed or feel that if you just keep using the same job search methods, even if they're not working, everything will 'come right' in the end.

On the other hand, you don't want to be too 'realistic'. Often, I find that a returner who claims that they're 'being realistic' is actually being pessimistic: too quick to dismiss the possibility of finding a rewarding job. The 'pessimistic realist' tends to believe the worst, quickly becomes disillusioned when they hit setbacks, and ultimately decides that returning to work is hopeless and not worth the effort.

Psychologist Sandra Schneider tells us that optimism and realism are not in conflict – we need both. Realistic optimists are cautiously hopeful that things will work out the way they want and will do everything they can to ensure a good outcome. As realists, they find out the facts and acknowledge the challenges and constraints that they face. Their optimism comes into play in their interpretation of ambiguous events. They recognise that many situations have a range of possible interpretations and choose a helpful rather than an unhelpful one. They give people the benefit of the doubt, are aware of the positives in their current situation and actively look for future opportunities.

Here's an example in practice. You send a 'getting back in touch' email to a former work colleague and, after a week, you still haven't had a response. It's all too easy to conclude that she just isn't interested in talking to you. But now consider other interpretations. Perhaps she's on holiday, or swamped with work and hasn't had time to reply, or the email has landed in her junk mailbox. Then, decide how to respond. You could contact her through a mutual friend or resend the email after a week. If she still doesn't respond, choose a realistically optimistic interpretation (such as, she's too busy) and focus on making other connections.

There is evidence that 'realistic optimism' can boost your resilience and motivation, improve your day-to-day satisfaction with life and lead to better outcomes. And be reassured that it's not about your genes: Professor Seligman's positive psychology research studies have found that we can all learn to be realistic optimists!

Here are some tips to help you become a 'realistic optimist' about your return to work:

1. Combine a positive attitude with a clear evaluation of the challenges ahead. Don't expect your journey to be smooth – you are likely to have setbacks – but trust that you have the ability to get yourself back on track.
2. Avoid dwelling on the negatives or jumping to overly negative conclusions. Recognise that this 'negativity bias' is a result of how our brains are wired (see Chapter 1).
3. Don't wait for the right time – it may never come. Simply taking action will move you forward.
4. Focus on what you can control, rather than worrying about what you can't (we will come to this again in Chapter 10).
5. If you think that lack of confidence is making you pessimistic, go back to Chapter 2.

Of course, there may just come a moment when you've been slogging away, doing all the right things, and still nothing. It's time to harness the 3Ps I mention above: positivity, patience and persistence.

When you have a low point, remind yourself of your motivations for returning, and read some success stories. Then take some practical steps to take care of yourself. Have a little break – a week off applications – and distract yourself with doing something fun in the time you get back.

Then consider changing tack slightly: take a course, find a skilled volunteer role, try something else from the 'routes back' list in this chapter. Doing something different can bring you new energy – and will put you in new situations where you may just get your 'lucky break'.

Don't forget your return-to-work support team. Call on them for a pep talk, for some perspective, for a brainstorm of some new ideas. Or just to blow off steam.

Remember that persistence does pay off. As one returner said, 'Every no takes you closer to a yes.' The right role for you is out there, as it was for all of these returners:

'I applied for so many jobs, hundreds of jobs, I thought I'd never get back to work. I assumed my career was over. I was thrilled and surprised to be accepted on to a returner programme after an 18-year break.' Darlene, business analyst, after an eighteen-year break

'Being back at work is exciting and challenging, and I am very glad I made the leap. I would advise anyone trying to get back to work to not give up!' Siobhan, medical records administrator, after an eighteen-month break

'I look back at this year and I cannot believe I am back! I feel so glad that the day that I have been waiting for – for so long – has finally come.' Alice, animator, after a three-year break

Summary

- You might feel as if you're sending your applications into a black hole. You're not imagining it: there are recruitment biases against career returners that you have to overcome.
- The good news: there are many employers who see the wealth of skills, experience and perspective that returners bring.
- Be targeted and creative. Look for returner programmes and other returner-friendly employers; look for opportunities with a built-in trial period; use your networks; consider freelance work; consider stepping-stone skilled volunteering.
- Mindset is the key to success. Remain curious, creative and open-minded in order to create your own lucky breaks. Aim for 'realistic optimism' and be patient and persistent.

'It doesn't matter how many years of experience you have, how good you are at your job, how many qualifications you have, you will still get rejected – a lot. You just have to accept this. See any interviews you get, or any small bits of work, as a bonus. They're going to help you to look good and sound better for your next interview. Think of a job search as a numbers game.' Mark, now back at work as a policy lead, after a four-year break

8

'Can I ask for what I want?'

How to Match Expectations and Negotiate for What You Need

Perhaps you're in the final round of interviews for a job or a returner programme. Or perhaps things have moved quickly and you've already been offered a role. You're excited to be so close to actually getting your career back. But now it's almost a reality, you realise that you've focused so much on selling yourself that you've parked the *practicalities* for too long. Can you make the job fit in with your life?

In this short chapter, I'll home in on how you can target the flexibility and salary you're looking for, striking the right balance between underselling yourself and expecting too much. The overall aim is a realistic compromise between your needs and the needs of the business.

Find flexibility

I've advised you, in previous chapters, against having too rigid an idea of what flexibility you need. This maximises your chances of finding a flexible working model that works for you and the team you're joining. However there's a balance here: you do need to be realistic about whether the job can fit in with the rest of your life. I have encountered some rather extreme cases at both ends of the spectrum. At one end, people who are so grateful to be offered a job that they take on a role which blatantly won't work with their commitments. They get very stressed and unhappy when the inevitable reality kicks in. At the other end, returners who feel really entitled and expect the working patterns of the role to revolve around them, and then are annoyed when they're not offered the flexibility they demand. Suffice to say – don't be either of these kinds of people!

It's important to have worked out in general terms what you actually need. Back to your career compass notes (Chapter 4)! Then, as you progress through the assessment stage for any role, make sure that you're checking for a match between what you want/ need, the flexible working culture, policies and norms of the company, and the demands of the particular role you are applying for.

We are often asked at Career Returners about when and how to talk about flexible working. This is role and culture specific, but I can share some general principles. First, I would suggest that you don't talk about flexibility at the application stage or in the first interview, unless the interviewer raises it. In these early stages, you need to focus completely on selling your motivation and fit for the role and the organisation.

Unless the recruitment process is very drawn out, the second interview or assessment stage is a good moment to raise the topic. If there are multiple rounds, you may wait a little longer, until you feel that you've got good buy-in. When the time feels right, ask first about what forms of flexible working are available for the role you're applying for, and whether these are taken up by existing team members, before talking about what could work for you.

Make sure that you ask for things that are reasonable and realistic, based on the opportunity and the organisational culture. Any flexible working needs to fit with the team and the business, as well as with you. Be open minded about alternative options and suggest a trial period if your manager has concerns.

Do go back to Chapter 4 and look at the content there about the different types of flexible working. Things have changed so much in the world of work – you might be surprised at what is possible!

'I was really worried about juggling the logistics of school runs and getting to work on time. My employer agreed to flexible working hours that suit my daily routine, so the logistics have not been too difficult.' Ellie, journalist, after a four-year break

'I started off thinking that part-time work was the only option that would work for me. With hybrid working, however, I can get the salary of a full-time role with the time at home that I was looking for.' Priya, policy advisor, after a two-year break

Negotiate your salary

Your salary will clearly relate to the level you are joining at. Returners often believe that they need to take a role many levels below their skillset and worth just to get back in the workforce.

However, as soon as your confidence returns and you've refreshed your skills, this lower-level role is unlikely to be a good fit – unless you have a clear rationale such as moving to a very different sector or taking a lower stress job.

In general, don't sell yourself short! Your career break does not inevitably mean that you must be penalised financially. What, then, can you do to become more confident at negotiating your salary first time back?

First of all, get clear on what salary you should be asking for. Collect up-to-date salary information upfront by researching the marketplace, to give you a benchmark of the salary range that you can reasonably target. Do be realistic – there is likely to be a range dependent on variables such as the size and nature of the business, the location, and how structured the internal salary grading is. If you have had a very long career break and will need extensive retraining, you also need to factor that into your thinking. Also, returner programmes may have a fixed salary band with limited possibility for movement – ask questions to understand the situation before you get into a salary conversation.

Once you have a realistic target salary range, be confident in the negotiation. Know your walk-away point, either where it is financially not viable for you, or where it is too far below market rates to be acceptable to you.

Do think in your negotiation about the broader picture. This is a good moment to look back to your trade-off triangle and remember that most job seekers have to compromise somewhere. If you're excited by the organisation and the role, and you have agreed a very flexible working pattern, you may be happy to accept a lower salary. Also, you could establish whether, despite a lower-than-ideal starting salary, there is good and quick potential for growth.

193

If you can't get to a starting salary or progression plan that you're happy with, and you don't have a clear rationale or urgency for taking the role, ask yourself whether this job is a match with your skills and the type of organisation you want to work for. Could it be a stepping stone to get a foot in the door, or would you be better off continuing your job search, with the confidence boost of having had a job offer?

Summary

- Aim for a match between the business needs and culture, and the flexibility you're looking for.
- Don't undersell yourself in salary negotiations, but recognise where compromise might be necessary for a mutually satisfactory outcome.

'After a long career break, it is too easy to feel like an employer is almost "doing you a favour" by employing you. Remember that no matter how rusty you may be, you are still a valuable commodity and have a lot to offer any workplace.' Maya, retail analyst, after a nine-year break

PART III

THRIVING BACK AT WORK

'Why do I keep waking in a panic at 4 a.m.?'

How to Prepare Yourself for Returning to Work

You've accepted a job, and you're thrilled to finally be returning to work. As the initial elation fades, though, doubts might start to creep in again. You lie awake worrying whether you're doing the wrong thing, whether you'll mess up because you really aren't up to doing the job, whether your family will cope without you, whether you've gone for the best opportunity, or whether you should have tried something else. As your start day gets closer, you realise that you have nothing to wear – in fact, you don't even know what people wear to work now.

You've come a long way since your 'shall I, shan't I?' worrying in Chapter 1, but now your anxieties have shifted. Your return to work has moved from being somewhere in the dim and distant future to an all-too-imminent reality.

Mandeep worked for many years in graphic design, but then, when her partner was diagnosed with cancer right after the birth of their daughter, she took a career break to look after them both. Three years later, her partner died. She decided not to go back to work immediately – she felt shaky, and her daughter was still so little. She continued her break for another four years, taking on a handful of freelance projects here and there, but mostly focusing on family and on building back her resilience. When her daughter started her third year at school, Mandeep realised that she was feeling stronger, more settled, and she reconnected with some old colleagues. She got a job offer almost immediately, and then, suddenly, her start date was approaching fast. 'Personally, I was in an absolute blind panic. In fact, I almost bottled it the week before. I almost just said "I can't do this!" I was stressing about how it was going to feel after seven years out. And, thinking, on top of that, I'm a solo parent now and it's just me and my daughter, and can I make that work? And do I really have the emotional stability to be "on form" every day at the office? I was overthinking all the time and I felt very isolated.'

After the initial elation of the job offer I find that returners often, a little further down the line (in Mandeep's words), 'panic'. Don't beat yourself up if this sounds like you too even without the heft of a bereavement, negative or mixed emotions in this final leg of your career break are not at all unusual. The main thing is to avoid them derailing you.

This chapter provides advice about how you can prepare yourself – practically, professionally and psychologically – for actually going back. I'll cover how to get yourself from job acceptance to feeling ready and able to confidently step through the door on day one.

Preparing practically

I'll take the practical side first, not least because one of my major pieces of advice is to start this preparation early. Ideally, don't wait until you get the job! Once you finally get an offer, things can happen very quickly, and you could be asked to start within weeks. You don't want at that moment to be scrambling around to find childcare or organise a care plan, cramming online courses, or begging friends to pick up your volunteer commitments. Although you may not be able to follow through to completion on some of these actions before getting a job offer, you can at least have put plans in place or settled some decisions, ready to hit 'go' when you accept the new role.

As a general principle, you need to start making time in your life for work. We see many returners trying to be superhuman, adding work into a schedule that is already too full. This can quickly lead to exhaustion and a feeling of failing all round. Don't let this be you!

Caring arrangements

Returning to work is not a solo effort. Having practical support networks in place is essential to ease some of the stresses when you return to work.

If you have children, good childcare can be the greatest enabler to being a happy working parent, from full-time care for younger children, to before/after-school care as they get older. Look into this as soon as possible after you start an active job search, to give yourself a good window to get this in place and your children settled before you start.

If you're a carer for a parent, a partner or another relative, similarly aim to research options for a care plan well in advance, and to understand how long it will take to get these in place.

Always make a contingency plan, as things *will* go wrong – and inevitably they will go wrong in those first weeks back at work. You're a single parent, the childminder is unwell, your father is on holiday – who will you call on? You might be lucky enough to have family close by, but for many returners, their relatives live far away. Talk to other local working parents about how they manage; perhaps you could agree to be each other's contingency plan, so that you don't feel bad about the last-minute phone call. Adopt the same degree of planning for any other caring commitments. A common tip from successful returners is to have a plan A, B and C!

If you set up this plan provisionally, as soon as you get the job, you can press the 'go' button. Once you're happy with your care arrangements, you can reassure yourself that your family will be well looked after. This is a good inner champion message (page 19) to counterbalance any feelings of guilt or your negative inner voice telling you that you're being selfish by going back to work.

As ever, avoid the perfectionism trap! Accept that you may not get to a solution you're totally happy with from the start. But 'good enough' is good enough! This is another 'test and learn' moment as explained on page 124: trial a solution to see if it works well and be ready to adapt if it doesn't.

Volunteer/community commitments

Are you one of the people on long career breaks who have taken on volunteering roles in a charity or in your local community? These may have become a very rewarding part of your life and, understandably, you're possibly reluctant to give them up. You feel a great sense of responsibility and don't want to let anyone down. However, you have to make space for work. So, if volunteering currently takes a large proportion of your time, you will probably need to cut down or completely hand over your responsibilities in order to make more time for work.

As you start an active job search, this is the moment to sound out other people, to find someone who is ready to take on your own commitments. As soon as you feel ready, start to hand over some of your responsibilities. Don't make this another thing to add to the last-minute list once you get a job.

Managing home life

We all know that looking after a family goes well beyond child-care, so if you've taken on full family management during your break, this is the section for you. When you get into an active job search, start to draw up a handover plan. The aim is to get other members of your household more engaged in domestic life and sharing the load. If you're a parent of school-age children, start to delegate more to them and encourage their independence. If you're the default taxi driver, still ferrying your older children around, let them get used to public transport (if that's possible in your geographical situation). Similarly, with your partner, if you have one, start to hand over and share out more of the home responsibilities.

If you're a parent, watch out that you don't fall into the trap of 'gatekeeping'. (Gatekeeping is classically 'maternal', but it can appear in parents of any gender who've taken on the bulk of the family and home responsibilities.) Gatekeeping plays out when you constantly check in on a task you've passed to your partner or children, because you want to ensure that they're 'doing it right'

201

(in other words, like you would do it). Then, you're critical if they don't do it exactly as you would. Does this sound familiar? If so, mentally mark when you're doing it and bite your tongue when the criticisms come into your head. Otherwise, you'll not only demoralise your family, but you'll also make it very hard to share responsibilities when you're back at work.

Clarifying priorities

This is the moment to decide your priorities or 'must-haves'. What are the things you feel you absolutely have to keep on doing? In other words, as one returner said, 'Work out what will hurt your heart if you give it up.' Get clear on these priorities, and then work out how you can delegate, hand over, or stop doing the other activities. If you need a little help handing things over, 'My week', below, can be a useful exercise.

Self-coaching exercise: My week – prioritise, delegate, ditch

Map out your current week, with all your commitments and activities.

	Monday	Tuesday	Wednesday	Thursday	Friday	Saturday	Sunday	Every day/ no particular day
Home								
Family								
Community/ Volunteer								
Self								
Other								

Decide where to focus your time, energy and attention, once you add employment into the mix. Which activities do you want/need to keep in your life, for family, others and yourself? What can you delegate to family or paid help? What can you stop doing, cut back on or pass on?

PRIORITISE: What are my must-haves?	DELEGATE: What can other people do?	DITCH: What doesn't need doing?

Back to Mandeep. She knew she wanted to do school drop-off every day for her daughter, but that would mean she had to stay late on some work days, so she booked after-school care for three days a week. She had been volunteering with a local children's sports team over the preceding eighteen months. She didn't want to give up entirely on something so rewarding, but knew she needed to scale back. She said she could still help out at weekend matches, but she found another volunteer to take on the scheduling and accounts. She also took on someone to do cleaning and laundry one day a week at home.

After taking these steps, the week before joining, Mandeep admitted, 'I was starting to convince myself that I couldn't possibly go back to graphic design and also juggle everything I needed to manage as a sole parent. Luckily, my employer seems to be

relatively flexible about my working hours, and I can work re-
motely two days a week. But I have also had to accept that I can't
do everything I did before. It was a hard pill to swallow, but I can't
give 100 per cent both at work and at home. Working out where
I can lower my expectations, what I can delegate and what I can
drop entirely was game-changing for my anxiety about returning. I
feel as though I have a plan now, and I'm sure things will become
clearer once I actually start. I have accepted that I may have to
make more changes if I still can't get the balance I want.'

Finally, don't forget to schedule a bit of time every week for
yourself. You may read that and think *what an indulgence* – or
even that it's not possible – but it is an essential part of your plan
in order to avoid overwhelm when you start work. This is how two
other returners carved out time in their busy schedules:

'I had to timetable what my week was going to look like both
at home and in work. And one priority was making sure that
my key things were there, like my exercise, my walks with
friends, the night out with friends that I was looking forward to
after the first four weeks. I made sure that was all part of the
plan and I really think that helped me.' Katia, nutritionist, after
a three-year break

'I like to get up an hour before everybody else so that I can do
some yoga and have a cup of tea and just set the scene for the
day, to feel a little bit on top of things. This way, I can carve
out some time at the beginning of the day, just for me.' Stacie,
veterinary nurse, after a nine-year break

Your style – appearance and image

Many career returners find it hard to decide what to wear on their first day and weeks back at work. Perhaps you have only a vague, aspirational idea – or perhaps no idea at all.

Aara described her thoughts on this: 'I want to fit in and look relevant. I also want to look credible and competent, and be taken seriously again. But both the world of publishing and my body have changed, I don't know where to begin.'

Don't dismiss these concerns about your appearance as frivolous. Deciding what to wear is not only about preparing practically, but also psychologically. Really, I could have put this style section under either heading.

How you dress and appear has a fundamental impact on how you feel. As a returner, buying a few new work outfits can help you to reconnect with your professional identity, thereby boosting your confidence. And there's more to this than looking professional: it's crucial that you feel comfortable in your clothes, that you feel 'like you' rather than as if you're acting a part. Cognitive psychologist Dr Carolyn Mair, who specialises in the psychology of fashion, explains that we find it stressful if we're out of sync with our outfits. That stress affects our confidence and means that we have less cognitive capacity to deal with the situations we find ourselves in. This is one reason why many successful people wear a 'work uniform' that they feel comfortable in, to free up mental resources for more important matters.

This makes sense to me, as I have my own work uniform. Since I founded Career Returners, I've always worn green when I'm in work mode. Green is our brand colour and, more importantly, it conveys the positive image of growth and change that I want the organisation to put across. Wearing a strong colour also makes me feel more confident, and it means that I stand out in a crowd, which helps at the events I attend or speak at. And I never have any problem with co-ordinating items in my working wardrobe!

I do want to flag that there are no strict rules on colour – colours have different cultural and individual connotations. It's about your personal preference, so consider which colours make you feel good, and make a conscious effort to wear them to elevate your mood.

There is even evidence that what you wear can impact your performance. Studies of 'enclothed cognition' (see psychology box below) suggest that if you associate what you wear with a particular symbolic meaning, that in turn can influence your mental performance in the associated area.

Psychology: Enclothed cognition

We all know that what we wear affects how we feel, but can it also affect how we behave and perform?

In a 2012 study, Adam and Galinsky tested this question using a white lab coat, a uniform associated with 'attentiveness and carefulness'. They tested a sample of people wearing a lab coat versus a control group, and found that the participants wearing a white lab coat performed better in attention-related tasks. The researchers delved deeper with a second experiment: one set of participants wore a lab coat and were told that it was a doctor's coat, and the other set wore the same lab coat, but this time it was described as a painter's coat. The people wearing the 'doctor's coat' performed much better in attention-related tasks than the people wearing the 'painter's coat'.

Adam and Galinsky termed this effect 'enclothed

> cognition'. The takeaway: performance is affected by the combination of the symbolic meaning of particular clothing and the physical experience of wearing that clothing.

The effect of our clothing is not just inward, though, it also works outward: it says things about you to other people. Inevitably, the way you dress will influence the first impressions that your new colleagues make of you (back to the halo effect in Chapter 6). Have a go at the coaching exercise below to get clear on how you want to come across in a work context, and think about how your clothes can convey those messages.

Self-coaching exercise: My target image

Think of three words to describe how you want to come across in a work context. You're aiming to define and pin down your desired image. To help with this:

1   Look back to your 'Which three words?' exercise in Chapter 6 (page 152) where you thought about how you wanted others to describe you, and see if you want to use some or all of those words here – it's a different angle here, so you might want different words.

2   These are some words that returners often use: assured, knowledgeable, professional, youthful, capable, expert, approachable, authentic, focused, current, creative, motivated, aspiring.

What's my desired image in three words?

1

2

3

Use these new three words as a litmus test for your existing work outfits, and to help you to choose any new outfits.

Show your 'look' to a few friends, to get their feedback and advice on whether you are achieving the image you're aiming for. You could also ask, if it feels appropriate to you, for feedback on your wider appearance, including hair and make-up.

Back to Aara's concerns about fitting in. In many countries and sectors, what people wear in a professional setting has changed significantly over the last decade. Do ask both your future employer and friends in your sector about current working norms. You can do some practical research too, such as looking on your new employer's social media, to see what their employees are wearing. Some returners have even stood outside their future work building at lunchtime to observe! This research will help you to set some guidelines for your own working wardrobe.

Now put your research together and look for clothes that sit in the intersection of your target image and your employer's norms. In this way, by feeling that you fit in while also feeling 'like you', your clothes will strengthen you for your return.

Aara chose capable, current and approachable as her three words. She got some help on what was 'current' from an ex-colleague and friend, who explained that people dressed much more casually now in publishing. She decided that she would trial wearing structured dark basics to help her to feel capable and competent. She liked the idea of creating a 'work uniform' to make her decisions easy day-to-day. But she also spent some time choosing colourful and original accessories to signal approachability, and because she felt it would make her feel more confident.

Ending on a practical note, you might be able to repurpose many or all of your previous work outfits. If you can afford it, updating your look with a few key items will help you to step into your new work identity. But don't over-invest before your first day. Give yourself the freedom to develop your image over time once you're back at work.

Preparing professionally

You're hopefully, even before a job offer, already some way down the track of preparing yourself professionally, having refreshed your knowledge ready for interviews and other assessments. As you approach your start date, now is the moment to identify any nagging worries that remain at the back of your mind (these are the ones that will keep you awake at 4 a.m.).

Tech

For many returners, it's the advances in day-to-day office tech that worry them. Before you have the job, get your preparation in by taking an upskilling course in common office software. There are many free self-directed learning courses, available online through open-access platforms, as well as free or low-cost local training options.

Once you have the job offer, but before starting the job, find out what tech platforms are used by your new employer for internal communication, video-conferencing and, if relevant, analysis and preparation. If you haven't already learned about these platforms, take an online course to get up to speed. It's also worth asking your employer if you can access their tech training modules to get updated before you start.

Sector changes

Are you feeling very disconnected from the latest developments in your profession or sector? It's normal to feel that you have huge gaps in your knowledge, particularly if you're starting work in a new country or sector. Set aside a few 'updating' time slots each week to tap into industry journals, professional associations, online articles and podcasts. In this way you will refresh your knowledge and pick up any new jargon and acronyms, and generally feel more connected to the area.

Once you have done some 'updating' groundwork, one of the best ways to get back up to speed is by talking to contacts in your field, asking about what's changed in the years since you left. You can fix these conversations with ex-colleagues, or anyone you got on well with when you were having exploratory networking and informational interview conversations. This helps to avoid the discomforting feeling that everyone is talking a new 'jargon language' in your first weeks back at work. Do also ask about what is the same – it can be very reassuring to find that so many things, in fact, have not changed.

Company culture and working norms

Find out more about your future employer by following their social media and the professional social media of your future team members. If you have any personal contacts at your new company, set up a conversation to ask about the culture and what it's like to work there. 'What would you have liked to know before you started at the company?' and 'What types of people tend to be successful at the company?' are good questions to get this discussion going.

Here's how two returners prepared in the final weeks before returning to work:

> 'I read up on the company and I did lots of revision. I did my homework just so that I felt like I knew the organisation I was going into. I dusted off my project management notes and refreshed myself on all that. I read up on the legislation and the requirements for the role I was starting. It wasn't stuff I was expected to know, and nobody was checking. I was just putting my head into that space to get myself in the right frame of mind.' Rosa, logistics manager, after a seven-year break

> 'I did a lot of online modules, various e-learning packages about things that were going to be relevant to the role. I did talk to other doctors who had done a similar job about what the role involved and what to expect. And I think that was helpful for feeling prepared.' Claire, orthopaedic doctor, after a four-year break

Professional introduction

Another important part of professional preparation is getting your introduction ready. In your first weeks you're likely to be meeting a number of new work colleagues. If you're in a larger company, and they don't know your background, one of their first questions will likely be along the lines of 'Where were you working before?'

As a returner, this is a tricky one to answer off the cuff. Do you say: 'I was working part-time in a local school'? Or 'I was at home'? Or 'I was at Microsoft – ten years ago'?

Self-coaching exercise: My professional intro

This is the moment to revisit and refine our trusty 'career break sandwich' framework (from Chapter 6). Once you're back at work, you can adapt parts 1 and 2 from your networking introduction and add the role that you're now doing. Aim to keep it really brief for your 'elevator intro', with a longer version for the team members you're working more closely with.

Professional background:

I am a/my background is/I worked for [add] years as [add]

Career break:

I took a career break for [add] years/months during which I [add]

Current role:

I'm now working within the [add] team, on [add]

Check that your current role logically flows from your professional background. If you're making a career change or pivot, briefly explain the change, bringing out relevant interests and values from your previous experience, so that your story doesn't sound disjointed. As before, practise your introduction. Try it out on a friend to get feedback and refine it. Then practise again – until you feel credible, convincing and authentically you.

This is the brief elevator intro that Mandeep developed: 'I've worked as a graphic designer since university, focusing on brand identity. My last job was as the creative lead in a start-up. I took a few years out to focus on my family, and now I've just started here in the marketing team.'

Preparing psychologically

Now to the (often neglected) psychological side of preparing to return. Don't leave your mental prep to the last minute or, even worse, ignore it entirely!

In the run up to their new job, many returners focus solely on the practicalities of getting everyone else ready. If you have continuing family commitments, it's easy to spend all your time on others: sorting out childcare or eldercare, meal planning, writing the household to-do list. You might manage to fine-tune the practicalities, but you're running a risk by not giving yourself time to think. By shelving any inner doubts until the last minute, you can end up feeling overwhelmed, and not in the right mindset when your start date comes around.

From Mandeep again: 'I do feel that being professionally ready is actually not as important as being personally ready, and in the head space to be clear about why it is you want to work and what it is you're looking to get from work.'

In Chapter 1, I highlighted William Bridges's transition model to help show why change is hard, and how the emotional transition as you adjust to a change is so unsettling. One of Bridges's key points is useful at this point in your return journey: every new beginning starts with an ending. And so now, as you approach the exciting new beginning of returning to work, you are also experiencing an ending – of your career break life.

This is a major transition point, which can ignite a lot of positive emotions: energy, excitement, anticipation, enthusiasm, perhaps relief, if you've been trying to get back to work for a long time or really need the salary. However, your life on career break probably had its fair share of joys (as well as its frustrations). And so, take time to reflect on what you will miss and accept the sense of sadness at what you're losing.

For some of you, the loss may be unlimited time with your children or your elderly parents. For others, it might be losing the autonomy to organise your day in the way that you wanted. In general, it will be casting aside the security blanket of your familiar life and daily structure, and stepping into an uncertain world. This uncertainty can revive your more negative emotions: self-doubt, anxiety, and perhaps guilt.

Given this mix of positive and negative emotions in this final leg, the ambivalence about returning that we covered in Chapters 1 and 2 might kick in again. And our negativity bias means that your mind will focus on the downsides – your 'Gremlins' are back! This churning of feelings is what wakes you at 4 a.m. and can make you want to flee from a job you were so happy to secure. Put yourself back in control by working through the 'Managing the "final leg" emotions' exercise, below.

Coaching exercise: Managing the 'final leg' emotions

Let's start with a coaching question: how are you feeling about going back to work? Pause and write down what comes into your head, starting each statement with 'I'm feeling ...'

How am I feeling about going back to work?

I'm feeling ...

I'm feeling ...

I'm feeling ...

I'm feeling ...

First, take a moment to look at the positive feelings you've written down. Allow yourself to experience them. Hopefully, you'll feel a smile coming to your face. Now, look at any negative feelings you've written down. The good news is: we already have the skills and tools to combat these. There are lots of things we've already covered in our journey back to work that you can revisit at this moment.

Unsure If you're feeling uncertain that you're doing the right thing, go back and remind yourself of your motivations to return ('Finding my why', page 32). Remember that this is a first step back; it doesn't have to be perfect. If it doesn't work out, you'll still be a step further forward in terms of rebuilding your skills and experience.

Anxious Try to pin this down further. What are you anxious about? Name your fears and doubts, and then you can start to tackle them, using the 'Balance the scales' exercise on page 15.

Guilty If guilt is kicking in, redo the 'Red flag or red herring' exercise on page 24. Remind yourself that work and family life can benefit each other: fulfilling work can give you more energy and a happier home life. Look for benefits, not conflicts. However, if you find a red flag, address it upfront with your employer.

Sad We've just talked about this one – acknowledge what you're giving up and the feeling of loss that comes with this. It'll then be easier to let go and move forward.

Self-doubt/loss of confidence The professional preparation we've already run through in this chapter can help to mitigate your self-doubts – reconnecting you with your professional self, and clarifying which strengths and experiences you would like to bring to your new role. Also, go back and look at the confidence-building tools I introduced in Chapter 2. Re-read your achievements list. Think about summoning courage to return rather than confidence, and remember that confidence builds through action. Once again, remind yourself that your skills are still there despite your break, even if your knowledge might be a little rusty.

Emotional support

As you prepare for your first day, bolster yourself with some emotional support. Spending time with your cheerleaders, those people around you who are championing your return, will increase your energy and enthusiasm for getting back to work.

Sharing your excitement and nerves about returning to work with family members will get them involved in your journey and encourage them to root for you, rather than just focusing on the inevitable changes that will come once you start work.

As you take the final steps towards your first day, here is advice from a few returners who are now thriving back at work, but who remember the last-minute fears and doubts:

'It's perfectly OK and natural for self-confidence to be on the lower side having not been at work for a long time. But believe me when I say that it will all come back and the world is changing at such a fast pace that even people who have been around for a long time are having to reinvent.' Kate, data scientist, after an eighteen-month break

'Believe in yourself. Keep telling yourself "I can do it. I have so many skills".' Greg, occupational psychologist, after a six-year break

'Remember that for every one thing you might have to remember to do, there is another skill that you are better at because of your break.' Linda, researcher, after a nine-year break

'Surround yourself with as much positivity as possible.' Lowri, fund manager, after a five-year break

Summary

- After the initial thrill of getting a job offer, you might find yourself nearly as/just as/even more anxious than you were at the start of your return-to-work journey. This is normal!
- You can, and should, start your returning-to-work prep well before you get your job offer – don't leave it until the last minute. Some things you won't be able to put into action before you have an offer or have set timings, but you can do the research.
- Practical prep includes sorting out caring arrangements, handing over volunteer or community commitments, and working out how you'll run your home life.
- If it all feels too much, map out your 'standard' week and then decide what you will prioritise, ditch and delegate.
- Plan your work outfits and appearance in advance – how you look feeds directly into how you feel, and how you come across to others, and how you perform.
- Psychological preparation is crucial too. Remember that this is a – difficult – transition moment. Try to pin down what emotions you're feeling, and revisit exercises from earlier in the book to help manage those feelings.
- Surround yourself with your supporters.

'Don't leave it until the last minute to prepare, or underestimate getting your head in the right place. That's just as important as sorting out logistics for everyone else in your life.' Mandeep, now back at work as a graphic designer, after a seven-year break

10

'Why do I feel like I'm failing at everything?'

How to Ride the Emotional Rollercoaster of Returning

There are lots of wonderful aspects to going back to work after a long break, and there could well be some tough setbacks or complications. It is rarely simply one or the other.

'My confidence started on a high, and then plummeted after a couple of weeks – I seriously feared I'd bitten off more than I could chew.' After a sixteen-year break, Leda hit her first day back at work full of hope, excitement and no small measure of relief. She'd been trying to get back to work for nearly two years, had applied for well over a hundred jobs without success and had started to believe that she was unemployable. When she eventually secured an HR job with a leading construction company, it felt 'like a dream'.

Her first week in the role was great. Everyone was very welcoming and she felt positive and well supported. She loved the feeling of waking up with a job to go to. But by the third week the excitement had worn off, and 'everything felt incredibly intense'. She was struggling to understand how all the new processes in such a big organisation worked – who did what, and where she fitted into the structure. She felt embarrassed to be 'asking so many stupid questions'. Everyone was still friendly but seemed so busy. She made a (minor) mistake in her first report and started to question her ability to succeed in the role: 'I could have done this project so easily before, why am I finding it so hard now?' She started staying up late to work, to try to 'keep up', once she'd put her children to bed.

Meanwhile, on the home front, she was hit by a childcare upheaval in week four, when a virus flared at school. She didn't feel that she could take time off herself to be at home and had to scramble around to find a friend who could help. Her children are telling her that they miss her being around, and her youngest has had a few meltdowns about going to school. Five weeks in, she feels on the verge of a crisis: exhausted and overwhelmed, and wondering if she's made a fundamental mistake: 'I feel as if I'm failing at home, in my new role, at everything. Perhaps I just can't make this work, after all.'

Sairose's emotional journey was different – she travelled in almost the opposite direction to Leda. Reflecting on her experience after five months back at work, she says: 'I was so worried before I started that I wasn't doing the right thing. That my carefully constructed life to manage my daughter's cystic fibrosis would collapse like a house of cards when I went back to work. I often felt close to tears in the early weeks, but in many ways it was so much easier than I had expected. I had a lot of support from my line manager and got up to speed faster than I ever thought I would. I did have to swallow my pride by asking lots of questions. But, by the second month, I felt my confidence slowly returning. I feel back to being me, which gives me so much more energy. My daughter has had a few wobbles, but she has settled well into her new routine a few months in. I think she likes me not being around so much to fuss over her!'

As you can see from the above, returning to work can be an emotional rollercoaster!

In this chapter, I'm going to talk through some psychological and practical tools to help you ride the ups and downs of this first six months – to help you thrive in this period and come out the other side, feeling truly 'returned'.

Let's start with a balanced perspective on what to expect, both the highs and the lows. First, a headline: overall, in my experience, after six months, the vast majority of returners say that they are happy to be back at work. Even if they had a tricky time adjusting, or if they feel they're not in quite the right role, they're still happy that they're well on the way to resuming their career. So, if you give yourself time to get through the wobbly transition period, you're very likely to be glad you persevered.

What to expect – the upside

The most tangible reward of working is, of course, getting a salary. This can be a huge practical relief if you've been struggling financially, and it can also give a strong psychological boost to your sense of self-worth. As Leda said: 'I love having my own money again and taking off some of the pressure about paying the bills.'

As I've talked about since Chapter 1, however, the rewards of work go far beyond the financial. For many returners, having a job title again – regaining their work identity – is the highlight. Others talk about the huge pleasure of daily achievements and working within a team, the joy of having a regained sense of meaning and purpose, the pleasure of feeling like a role model to their children, the satisfaction of being more intellectually challenged.

> 'I love putting on my work clothes and heading into the office, it gives me such a buzz to be back in the working world.' Susanna, finance manager, after a seven-year break

> 'It was a wonderful feeling when I delivered my first solo project after going back, and my manager loved it ... I hadn't been that proud of myself in such a long time.' Divya, software engineer, after a seven-year break

> 'Now I'm back at work, I'm really happy and enjoying every minute of it. It feels great to be working in an environment where I am constantly stimulated.' Bettina, marketing manager, after a six-year break

> 'I'd forgotten how much I loved being in a team, bouncing ideas around.' Maria, government administrator, after a ten-year break

> 'I thought I'd be exhausted, but I honestly feel better – less foggy, more energetic.' Chris, librarian, after a three-year break

What to expect – the downside

Starting back at work is, of course, not all rosy. Many successful returners admit that they had to persevere through a fairly painful transition period in the early months. Your experience could be

223

wobbly, like Leda's, with a lot of lows to navigate before you emerge truly energised and confident.

> 'There were days when I just wanted to chuck it all in. It all felt too hard and stressful, and I think I missed the control I used to have over my days.' Mark, policy lead, after a four-year break

> 'I'd wanted to get back for so long. But the working world felt so different, and everyone seemed so much younger than me. I really wondered if I had left it too late to go back.' Rita, project manager, after a six-year break

To put this discomfort into perspective, do cast your mind back to your previous working life. Finding the start of any new job daunting is totally normal, particularly if it's with a new employer. Many (non-returner) job switchers have a crisis during the first few months, questioning whether they made the right move. It's not easy to navigate a new work culture and perhaps a new role, start again from scratch with building up your internal networks, and get to grips with a whole new set of company jargon and acronyms. Now, factor in being a returner, when you feel even further out of your comfort zone. It's not at all surprising that it can take a while to get into your stride.

You've come a long way, but you're not yet out of the uncomfortable in-between stage. You have already made the most obvious external change in the return-to-work journey – you have started your new job and taken on the job title that comes with it. But your inner, psychological return-to-work transition takes longer – it's not an overnight transformation. Be prepared to hang in there a while longer before you reach your new beginning, with your professional identity fully 'returned' and confidently owning your job title.

Everyone moves at their own pace, so be patient with yourself. From my experience, this identity shift is more likely to take a few months than a few weeks. Also, watch out for an emotional dip about a month in – this is very common, occurring at the moment when the initial excitement fades and long-term reality kicks in.

The first months back at work can be even trickier to navigate if you're also going through a major transition at home. Often, I've seen that it's not the work itself that feels toughest for a recent returner. It's something happening in the background: a divorce turns messy, a child gets ill or struggles with the change, or a caring team is unreliable.

I've put together this 'Return-to-work emotional transition' model, to give you a feel for the typical rollercoaster of positive and negative emotions that you might experience during the first six months.

The return-to-work emotional transition

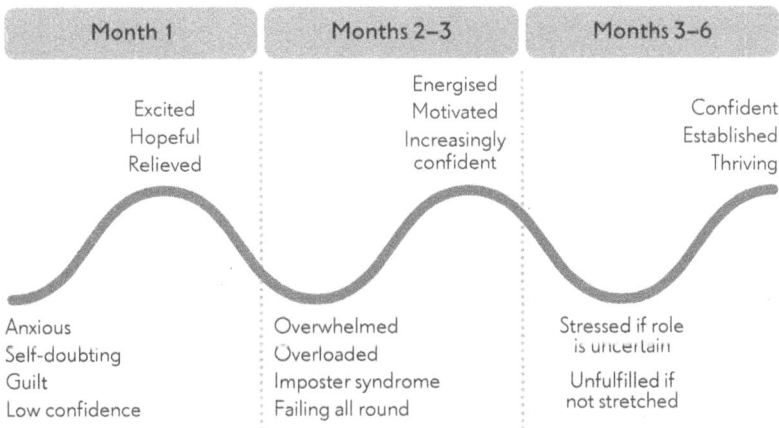

Month 1	Months 2–3	Months 3–6
	Energised	
Excited	Motivated	Confident
Hopeful	Increasingly	Established
Relieved	confident	Thriving

Anxious	Overwhelmed	Stressed if role
Self-doubting	Overloaded	is uncertain
Guilt	Imposter syndrome	Unfulfilled if
Low confidence	Failing all round	not stretched

These up-and-down emotions, combined with very real practical challenges, might make you feel as though you want to walk away from this new chapter and go back to your career break life. I encourage you to hang in there, if you can, so that you can make a clearer decision once you're through the transition stage.

Fortunately, there are many things you can do to smooth the transition for yourself, and I will lay these out below. As in previous chapters, I'll start with some *mental* tools, to get your mind in the right place, then I'll move on to more *practical* tools and techniques. I can't guarantee you an easy ride, but I can assure you that if you work through the suggestions below, you're likely to get through the neutral zone faster, and out into your own positive new beginning.

Mental tools and techniques to help you through the transition

Getting yourself in the right mindset can make all the difference to your experience in the early months back at work.

1 Embrace realistic optimism

We've talked about 'realistic optimism' before, in Chapter 7, in the context of approaching your return-to-work job search with a helpful mindset. Adopting a realistically optimistic mindset once you're actually back at work is crucial too. It makes all the difference to your job and life satisfaction, and it has a major impact on how successful you are in your new role. This is particularly apparent in returnship programmes, where we see that it is often the participants with a more solution-focused, positive approach who receive a job offer at the end of the placement period.

How, then, do you apply 'realistic optimism' to your new role? The key is to approach it with a positive outlook, as this will help you to stay creative and open-minded, to build strong connections with your colleagues, to maintain your motivation and resilience and (as Richard Wiseman proved, as described on page 183) to make your own luck. Do read or listen to some of the success stories on the Career Returners website and podcast, to build up your sense of hope and optimism.

Don't be blindly optimistic, however. Temper your positive thinking with a dose of realism: recognise that things won't always go your way, and be prepared for setbacks. When problems come up, be ready to work with your employer, colleagues, family and friends to find solutions.

A significant part of approaching your role with realistic optimism is to do with setting realistic expectations: expectations of your manager, the job, the organisation. You'll know from your previous experience that the world of work is not perfect, line managers are not perfect, and business situations change rapidly. No job is amazing in every way, nor custom-designed for you. Even the best-structured returner programme can't iron out all the difficulties you might encounter. Make sure that any frustrations you have don't turn into complaining – you don't want to be marked out as a chronic grumbler! I'm not suggesting passive acceptance, but more to adopt a proactive attitude, where you look for solutions rather than drowning in the problems.

'Remind yourself that, like with all opportunities, there are ups and downs. Keep a mindset of positivity – seize the day and be honest about the support you need to make it work.' Diana, insurance underwriter, after a fifteen-year break

Just as crucially, set realistic expectations of yourself. Being realistic about how quickly you can get up to speed will reduce the stress you're putting on yourself, which will make you feel more satisfied and, in turn, it is likely to lead to more positive outcomes.

> 'Be patient with yourself. Play the long game. It takes time to establish yourself in your new role and team. Don't put pressure on yourself to hit the ground running on day one and be completely up to speed by month one.' Sam, electrical engineer, after a ten-year break

> 'Prepare to make stupid mistakes. Don't expect to know everything immediately.' Darlene, business analyst, after an eleven-year break

If you're struggling to set realistic expectations of yourself, here are a few tips:

1. See your return to your career as a learning process. Accept that you won't know everything all at once. Look back at the concept of a growth mindset from Chapter 2.
2. Practise the art of saying 'not yet'. For example, 'I'm not fully up-to-speed on that legislation yet' or 'I'm not familiar with that process yet'.
3. Encourage yourself to pay attention to the positive feedback you receive, just as much as any negative comments.
4. If you are still beating yourself up for not progressing faster, look back at the sections in Chapter 1 on negativity bias and being your own inner champion.

2 Tackle imposter syndrome

It's very common as a returner to experience 'imposter syndrome'. You might well be in a very different job or sector from your pre-break roles, and the workplace has most likely changed. You're finding your way around different routines, procedures and workplace norms. There's still a gap between the professional person you'd like to be and how you view yourself right now. In summary, you're well out of your comfort zone.

Sairose hit imposter syndrome in the early weeks back at work. 'I felt like I couldn't keep up with what everyone was talking about. I was afraid that I'd say the wrong thing and my manager would realise that I wasn't really up to the job after all.'

Imposter syndrome is characterised, as for Sairose, by the feeling that you don't deserve to be where you are, and that you're going to be found out. It's helpful to know that this is perfectly normal: studies have found that over 80 per cent of people are hit by impostor syndrome at some point, with career shifts as a typical trigger.

Psychology: Imposter syndrome

'Imposter syndrome' is another one of those terms, like 'perfectionism', that has made its way out of psychology and into everyday language. But what exactly does it mean?

In 1978, psychologists Pauline Rose Clance and Suzanne Imes studied 150 high-achieving women, and described three characteristic features of what they called 'imposter phenomenon':

---

1   You think others have an inflated view of your abilities.
2   You fear your true abilities will be found out and you'll be seen as a fraud.
3   You attribute your success to luck or external factors rather than your own ability.

Follow-on studies have found that these thoughts are incredibly common, and not just among women. For example, in 2020 a systematic review by Bravata and colleagues found that up to 82 per cent of men and women struggle with imposter syndrome at some point – but, mistakenly, they often see themselves as the 'only one' having these feelings.

When imposter syndrome rears its head, here's how you can ward it off:

1. Don't downplay your achievements before and during your break, or once you're back at work. Internally, focus on the part your strengths and actions have played in your successes to date. Externally, avoid attributing your previous career progression, or getting your new role, to luck. Being too humble can be harmful, especially if you're already feeling low in confidence.
2. Identify your imposter thoughts ('I'm not up to this', 'Someone else could do this much better than me'). Recognise that they are just thoughts, related to your low confidence and anxiety, rather than accepting them as the reality about your actual abilities. Do not accept your self-doubts as evidence that

you're not up to the job – instead, reframe them as a normal and temporary effect of moving out of your comfort zone.

3. Confidence comes by doing, so search out ways to build up your experience again. Once you have the 'first times' out of the way – the first meeting you speak at, the first report you write, the first presentation you give – you'll feel much more confident the second time around.

4. Set realistic goals. Recognise that you're not going to be an expert straight away.

5. Remind yourself that making mistakes is inevitable if you're doing new things. Life is about learning!

3 Avoid perfectionism

A word again to the perfectionists out there, particularly those with continuing caring responsibilities or health issues. In your pre-break career, you may have given nearly 100 per cent to work. You could make it your top priority and work as many hours as it took to get to the best possible outcome. In your career break life, you may then have switched to giving your all to your family and home, applying equally high standards to your non-working life.

Now, back at work again, this approach is untenable. You just cannot give 100 per cent to work and 100 per cent at home – nobody has 200 per cent to give!

Your new aim is to be 'good enough' in multiple areas of your life, rather than outstanding in just one. This is easier said than done for a perfectionist. Compromise can too easily feel like a failure.

Consider Leda, who had so much upheaval at home in the early weeks, but who still desperately wanted to be 'perfect' at work: 'I beat myself up mentally for every small mistake I made at work. I wanted to do everything right, to prove that the break had had no impact on my ability and that I wasn't out of touch.' We see this internal pressure a lot with returners – and it can lead to dissatisfaction, and burnout.

Here are some ways to help you to understand that 'good enough' can be 'good enough':

1. Recognise that getting to 'good enough' in multiple areas of your life can be framed as high achievement in itself.
2. See compromise as a necessary part of having a full and interesting life.
3. Rethink your definition of success. What does success mean to you now? Is it all about achievement at work, status or money? Or can you move to a broader definition, such as 'leading a full and fulfilling life'?

In the end, it was a friend who helped Leda to put things in perspective: 'She reminded me that I had already accepted that there is no perfection in parenting. I now needed to take this lesson to my job, as there's also no perfection in work. For me that was a really invaluable lesson.'

Practical tools and techniques to help you through the transition

The success of your return to work does not hinge, of course, entirely on mindset. You cannot always just think things to be better! So let's move on now to some practical steps that you can take.

1 Focus on what you can control

Spending too much time worrying and feeling frustrated about things we cannot change leads, inevitably, to high levels of anxiety and makes us feel passive and drained. Examples of these 'unproductive' worries and frustrations as you return to work might include:

- 'The organisation doesn't give enough support to new joiners.'
- 'My manager isn't very empathetic.'
- 'There's too much company bureaucracy.'
- 'Will I get made redundant if there's a restructure?'
- 'Do my young colleagues think I'm too old to be part of their team?'

One powerful way to manage your return-to-work anxieties is to turn your attention and energy towards the things you *can* control or influence, where you can take action to mitigate your worries. Use the 'In or out of my control' exercise to help with this. Examples of these 'productive' worries, with an idea of a related action, include:

- Worry: I'm struggling with the tech. Action: ask for extra training.
- Worry: I'm not sure how to succeed in the public sector. Action: seek out a mentor.
- Worry: I'm feeling very unhealthy. Action: create weekly meal plans.
- Worry: My after-school care is too expensive. Action: investigate options for lower cost alternatives.
- Worry: Have I sufficiently shown what I am capable of doing? Action: speak to your manager about taking on work that stretches you more.

Self-coaching exercise: In or out of my control

1   Write down a list of all the things that are worrying or frustrating you in the table below.

2   Put a tick in the relevant column, dependent on whether you can take any action to manage or influence the outcome.

Worries and frustrations	In My Control (productive) I can take action to manage or influence the outcome	Out of My Control (unproductive) I can do nothing to manage or influence the outcome

3   Identify whether you're spending most of your time worrying about things you can't control and, if so, consider the effect this is having on your energy levels. Commit to yourself to refocus on what is within your control.

4   For the worries and frustrations that are within your control, list at least two related actions you can take.

Worries and related actions

Worry	Action

Leda loved the 'In or out of my control' exercise. She quickly identified that she was spending far too much time thinking about things she had no power over: worrying whether her children would get sick again, whether her brain really had deteriorated, and whether all the moving parts of the project she was working on would get delivered on time. She realised that she just needed to park these things, because they were out of her control, and the anxiety was making her feel exhausted. She also identified a key worry that was within her control: not getting enough sleep and therefore becoming burnt out, so she made a plan to work on her work–life equilibrium. She also realised that there were far more things that she could influence, if she summoned her courage to act (back to courage!). She asked her manager if they could talk through the mistake she'd made. Her manager gave her some helpful advice to make sure that it wouldn't happen next time, as well as reiterating the other positive feedback he'd already given her. She also asked her manager if they could allocate her a 'buddy' within the team, who could help her to understand the internal processes and answer her 'stupid questions'. At the end of this, she said, 'I feel so much better now, it's great to feel that I'm taking more charge of things.'

2 Take charge of your own story

I've already talked a few times – in both the last chapter and in Chapter 6 – about the importance of a strong introduction.

Own your story – don't leave it to your manager to introduce you to people. They may not talk about you and your career break in the way that you'd like. I remember one manager introducing an experienced banking returner as someone who 'we're helping back to work after looking after their kids'. Don't risk this happening to you! Use the 'Career break sandwich' introduction you developed in the last chapter when you meet your team and other colleagues to express your credibility and enhance your confidence. Remember the halo and horns effect (Chapter 6) and the importance of making a positive first impression.

3 Create clear objectives and feedback processes with your manager

You may have a very organised line manager, who has put processes in place from the beginning to support your transition. Or you may well not, and it might be up to you to make this happen. Whichever scenario you're looking at, make sure you take an active part in making this relationship work for you both:

1. Agree clear objectives for the first three to six months, with sub-goals to check on progress week by week.
2. Put in regular meetings where you can get feedback on what you're doing well and how you can improve, and any training needs.
3. Ask for immediate feedback after important meetings or deliverables.

It can be hard to receive negative feedback, but avoid being defensive – talk about what you can learn and how you can improve.

4 Build a support team

I talked about building support at home in Chapter 9. Now is the time to do the same at work. If you try to work everything out on your own, you risk becoming overwhelmed and slowing your progress.

If you're on a structured returner programme, you're probably benefitting from a framework of support, which might include a buddy in your team, a mentor and coaching. If not, don't struggle on solo: create your own support structure. Ask your manager if they could nominate a 'buddy' in your team, to help you with day-to-day questions. Or take a 'do it yourself' approach: identify a friendly team member or two and ask if they wouldn't mind giving you a rundown on the new tech or processes you're grappling with. Just swallow your pride and explain you're a bit out of practice after your break.

It's also important to identify the key people in your team and the wider organisation who can help you to succeed. They may be the people with who you interact day-to-day, or they may be more senior people who you wouldn't come across much in the ordinary course of things. Ask your manager to make some introductions early on, so that you can set up initial conversations. To build wider networks, attend company events and join any relevant employee resource groups (such as parents/carers networks). One aim of this networking is to make connections with more senior people outside your line-management structure. They might take on an informal mentoring role, helping you to navigate the organisation's culture. Equally, over time, they could become your advocates in identifying future opportunities, and therefore influential in your career progression.

5 Write a return-to-work journal

Every week, note down the things that you've done well and what you have learned. Include any verbal or written feedback. Celebrate all the wins, big and small, to build your confidence and get a concrete sense of how much you're progressing.

Keeping a journal over the first six months has multiple benefits. It's a great way to track your achievements. It can also be a useful place to jot down your thoughts and feelings on a daily or weekly basis, or at key moments. Particularly on those days when your head feels full to burst, getting your worries out and onto paper can help to put them into perspective. But don't forget to put down positive emotions on a good day, too – you can look back at them on not-so-good days, to remind yourself of the upsides of returning to work.

Sairose found her journal helped her to focus on what she was doing well. 'I created a page for "positive feedback" and jotted down everything encouraging anyone said or wrote to me, from a simple "Great point" in a meeting to more formal praise for my first presentation. When I filled a few pages after six weeks in, it felt brilliant!'

Find your working equilibrium

Finally, but crucially, to the last characteristic that divides happy from struggling returners: feeling balanced rather than constantly stressed. Though, having used the word 'balanced', I should say that I am not keen on the overall term 'work–life balance'. It suggests that work and life are different and at odds with each other. And that there's a 'one size fits all' solution of spending equal time on work and home, which is not what we're aiming for. I prefer the term 'working equilibrium'.

What is working equilibrium?

- An inner state of feeling balanced rather than overwhelmed.
- Personal and individual, relating to our personalities and circumstances.
- A satisfactory integration of the various areas of life inside and outside work, in a way that works for you and is in line with your priorities.
- The way in which you allocate all your personal resources, not just your time, but also your energy and your attention.
- Fluid and changeable. We all move in and out of equilibrium. Balance isn't a goal to achieve, it's an ongoing process of 'balancing'.
- Best evaluated over a period of time. It is better to measure whether you felt in balance over the past month than over the last twenty-four hours.

Self-coaching exercise: My resources-balance wheel

This is an exercise which I've developed from the common coaching tool of the Life-Balance Wheel. It will help you to think about whether you are allocating all your resources (your time, your energy and your attention) in line with what is most important to you. See the example at the end to help you to complete the exercise.

1   Identify the six to eight areas of your life that are most
    important to you (for example, work/family/friends/exercise/
    hobbies/volunteer work).

2   Write each of these on a spoke of the wheel, as in the example
    on page 242.

My resources-balance wheel

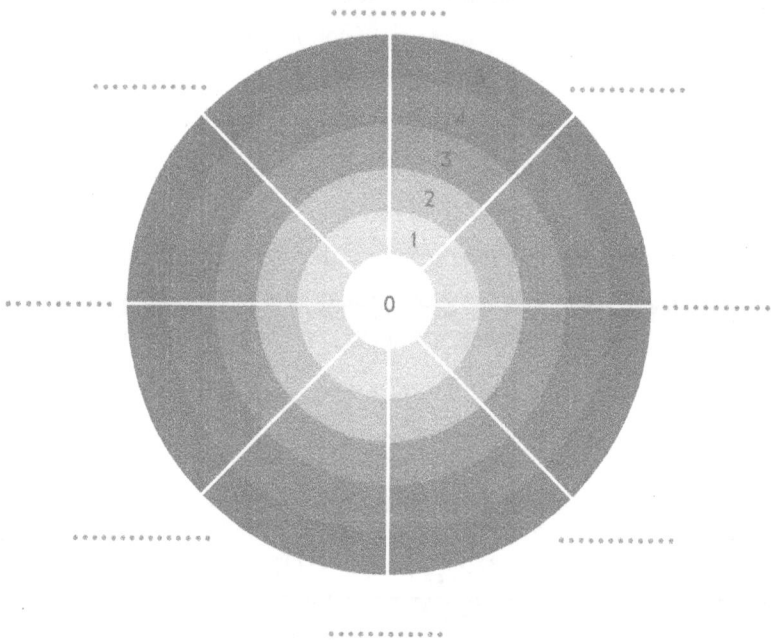

3   For each area, mark a cross on the spoke according to the
    amount of time, energy and attention you are giving to it at the
    moment (0 = none, 5 = very high).

4   Join together the crosses and look at the picture.

5   Does the balance across different areas of your life, as represented here, feel good to you? You will probably notice that the shape you've created is jagged, not even – that is, that you are giving more of your time, energy and attention to some areas than others. This is typical, and a round circle is not the ideal to aim for. What's important is to consider: are there areas of your life where you want to dedicate less of your resources and/or are there areas of your life where you want to dedicate more of your resources?

6   If you decide that you want to make a change, mark in a different colour on your wheel where you'd like to target. Perhaps you'd like exercise to move from a one to a three, or volunteer work to move from a five to a two. Remember that this is reflective of your priorities right now, you have the flexibility to change.

7   Write down two or three small actions you can take to narrow these gaps between where you are and where you want to be.

Actions to narrow the gaps

1.

2.

3.

Resources-balance wheel – an example

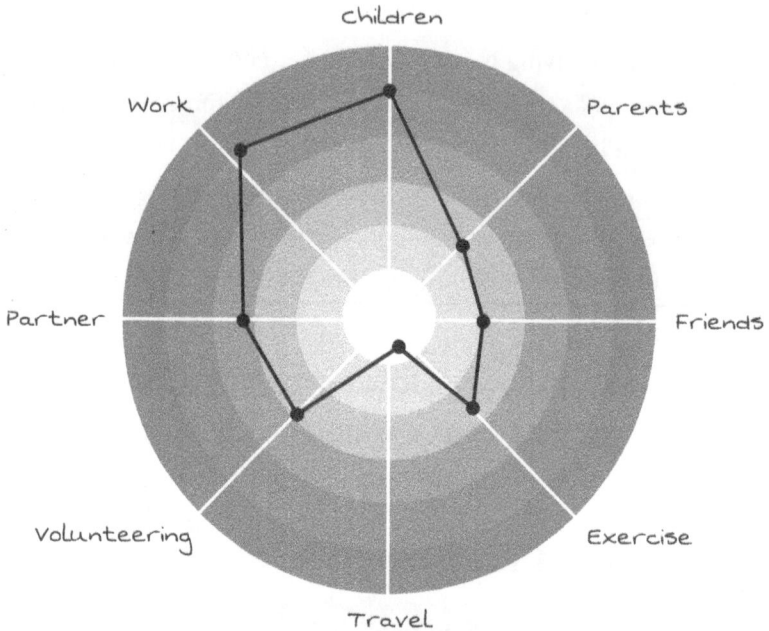

I say write down 'small' actions in the resources-balance wheel exercise, and I mean it. I know that everything in your life is finely tuned, and you cannot just throw things up in the air. One of the most powerful concepts in improving your equilibrium is the concept of making 'tweaks'. Rather than major changes, which are hard to implement and easy to put off, these are small actions that are manageable enough to fit into a busy week and that you can start doing straightaway.

We all move in and out of balance, with certain triggers that push us out of balance and small actions that can help us to get back in balance. Proactively identifying and making these 'balance restorer' tweaks can make a big difference to how calm and in control you feel. Over time, you can make them into sustainable habits, to improve your mood or stress levels on an ongoing basis.

Self-coaching exercise: My balance restorer tweaks

What are the small things that you can easily do, given the constraints you have, to restore your balance?

List between three and five 'balance restorer' tweaks that you can make, at work or home. Some examples of balance restorers are:

- Blocking out thirty minutes of quiet time in the week to think and plan.
- Blocking out five minutes of thinking space between meetings.
- Taking micro breaks every hour.
- Blocking time in your diary for a fun activity each week.
- Blocking time in your diary for enjoyable exercise each week.
- Switching off work email notifications.
- Putting your working hours on your email sign-off.
- Spending time with friends who energise you.
- Going for a half-hour walk in nature once a week.
- Listening to music on your commute.
- Not eating lunch at your desk – even if you move to a different part of the building, that's a change of scene! (Although going outside is better, if you can.)
- Do come up with your own tweaks too!

My balance restorers

1.

2.

3.

4.

5.

Highlight the smallest, most achievable tweak that you can do this week – and do it!

Then add the others into your daily life slowly, one by one. Aim to do a small number regularly, embedding each one as a habit, rather than trying to do too many at once.

Work–life separation or integration

The rise of flexible and hybrid working is definitely a good thing: it opens doors for people who cannot commit to being at a desk, in the office, during rigid core hours. For some of us, though, it creates a new problem: the blurring of boundaries between work and home. Trying to answer emails while you cook dinner; your dog bursting in when you're in an online meeting; the feeling, in general, of never being able to switch off fully from either home or work responsibilities but wearing both hats all the time.

Professor Ellen Kossek's research (see psychology box below) has shown that some of us ('integrators') thrive with this lack of boundaries, whereas others ('separators') really dislike it. There's no right or wrong way to work, the key to improving your working equilibrium is to understand your personal preference. If your current way of working is out of sync with your preference, think of small and achievable changes you can make to work in a way that better suits you.

Psychology: Work–life boundary style

Professor Ellen Kossek and colleagues carried out a quantitative study of teleworkers in 2006, followed over several years by interviews of a range of employees, including management consultants and factory workers. In 2007, Kossek and Lautsch identified two main 'work–life boundary management styles', relating to personal preferences:

1 **Separators**, who prefer their work and personal lives to be separate. They compartmentalise. They like clear boundaries and defined work schedules so that they can keep specific times in the week for work and specific times for home life. They want to switch off when they're outside of working hours.

2 **Integrators**, who are happy to combine work and personal activities and roles, and blur the boundaries. They switch easily between tasks, and they enjoy blending their work and home worlds, moment to moment.

A 2021 review by Desrochers and colleagues of follow-on research on this topic, reported that each style involves different trade-offs and that personal preferences fall on a spectrum from extreme separation to extreme integration. In general, individual wellbeing improves when a person has more control to flex their working patterns in line with their preferences.

Before I set up Career Returners, I ran a series of workshops for doctors on this topic: working equilibrium. Many were struggling with balancing families (parent care and/or childcare) with their demanding career. As we talked, it became clear to me just how stressful – and also how rigid – their jobs are: set and punishing hours, and the highest of stakes. We discussed at length the idea of tweaks. One doctor, a month after the workshop, told me that instead of walking through the hospital (which she had to do many times a day, end to end, visiting different wards) she now, when she could, walked around the hospital, outside, to get some fresh air. Another doctor told me he had stopped checking work emails on his commute home but listened to podcasts instead. This helped him to mark the boundary between work and home. Yet another loved reading but felt she had no time for it any more. She decided to read a few pages of an absorbing novel between operations, and found it was a quick way for her to regain her equilibrium in a stressful day.

You can make these tweaks both proactively and reactively. Get to know the early warning signs of when you're getting out of balance – perhaps losing your temper, or finding it hard to sleep. That's the moment consciously to take action to regain your equilibrium, using your 'balance restorers'. If these doctors can do it, then you can too!

Leda, knowing that she wanted to get to know her organisation better, combined that aim with the tweak of getting away from her desk, and resolved to ask a colleague to go out to get lunch with her once a week. She also set herself an absolute limit of 9 p.m. for working: 'I knew that I wasn't doing good work after that time anyway, and that if necessary I should go to bed earlier, and get up a little earlier to finish things off.' And once a week, on the way to work, she got off the train a stop early to walk the rest of the way. 'I always feel better, more energised, when I've moved my body a bit before sitting at my desk!' She had felt, before starting this process, that she couldn't possibly re-jig her precarious balance between work and home or add anything new to the mix – but with the idea of tweaks, she found that a few small changes did make a big difference.

At the end of three months Leda realised that life was getting much easier. After six months she described herself as 'thriving'. 'I just had to grit my teeth and ride it out, but I'm so very happy that I stuck with it. I'm back in my professional stride now!'

Summary

- The first weeks and months back at work as a returner can be a real emotional rollercoaster: huge upsides, and a lot that is hard. Remember, you are not yet out the other side of Bridges's neutral zone – this is all normal.
- Mentally, embrace a mindset of realistic optimism, resist imposter syndrome, and avoid perfectionism.
- On the more practical side, examine how much energy you're expending worrying about things you can't control, and take action where you can with the things that are worrying or frustrating you.
- Other practical actions might be seeking support, asking for clearer feedback and finding your working equilibrium.
- See if you can set aside the things that you cannot control or influence – spending too much time with these things is not good for your mindset.
- Maintain working equilibrium by mapping out, and seeing if you can slightly re-balance, your life-balance wheel.
- Embrace the idea of tweaks: tiny actions and habits to reduce stress and improve your balance.

'Be patient with yourself. Getting back into your career is like re-learning anything you used to be familiar with, it takes time. Do it at your own pace.' Leda, now back at work as an HR business partner, after a sixteen-year break

11

'Can I stop saying that I'm a returner now?'

How to Go from Returner to Returned

Y ou've been six or so months back at work, and suddenly, one day, you realise that you're no longer questioning whether you can do what you did before – you're just doing it! You're on top form. You're not only doing it, but also you are *confidently* doing it. You've shed your imposter syndrome. You no longer pause when someone asks you what you do – you say, without missing a beat, 'I'm a ... teacher/software developer/engineer/marketing manager/lawyer/investment manager/fundraiser/ ...' And it feels comfortable, and true.

You have not forgotten your career break – it is still a fundamental part of who you are. But you can appreciate, with a new perspective, how all the experiences you've had in life have made you stronger than ever now that you're back at work.

We come back now, full circle, to where we started – to William Bridges's transition model (see Chapter 1). You have taken a long journey – from the 'ending' of your career break, through the 'neutral zone' of finding and starting a new role and the identity transition that's come with that, and now out the other side, into your 'new beginning'. From Returner, to Returned!

The end?

I'm sure you'll still have wobbles every now and then. We all have them. Especially if you've had a particularly long break, when six months back can feel like just a drop in the ocean. Give yourself time to adjust. Don't beat yourself up for making a mistake, or start to panic if you don't feel that you're fully back to where you were before, or if the role just isn't feeling quite right.

This first job back might not be the ultimate role for you. That's OK. You're back in the game and developing new skills, experience and networks. You're on a stepping-stone path back to where you want to be. Be patient, and avoid being the team complainer, a source of negative energy. But don't sit still and stagnate. Take time to reflect on what's *not* working for you. Use the principles we've worked on together in this book, and the tools you've gleaned, to manage your career actively. Am I using my strengths? Am I working in an organisation that fits with my values? Am I getting the freedom and encouragement to thrive within my team? Am I finding a sustainable work–life equilibrium? Then work out the actions that you can take. If it's your job itself that isn't a great fit, can you craft it to make a better match for you, or can you get involved in a new project? If you're not happy in the team or with your manager, can you find another opportunity within the organisation? Even if you end up leaving, remember that you're not starting from scratch again. You're so much further down the road than you were. You've refreshed your skills and experience, and you have a springboard from which to find a great job the next time around.

This may not be 'The End' for you (is it ever?), but it is the end of an important chapter: your return-to-work transition. Take a moment to celebrate just how far you've come. If you did keep a journal, as I suggested in Chapter 10, and you wrote down how you felt at key moments, go back and look at those notes now. Can you see how much progress you've made?

I also want you to take a moment once again to recognise the value of your career break and all that it's brought you. Think about the ways in which it has made you better and stronger now you're back at work. I've talked around this before, but sometimes it's not possible to appreciate this properly until you are fully established in your new identity and can look back with some perspective. It is something I hear from returners a lot – months and even years down the line: from doctors, who value their increased empathy with patients; from IT specialists, who before were technically focused but now feel they have better people-management skills; from people in advertising and consumer goods' sectors, who say that they have a much better understanding of their target audience now that they have been on the other side of the fence.

So, the answer to the question, 'Can I stop saying I'm a returner now?' is a resounding *Yes!*

Own your career break

Don't hide your career break – make it part of your career story. In doing so, you can play an important part in encouraging and inspiring the returners coming up behind you. Don't forget the journey you've taken to get here. By sharing and talking about your career break, the ups and downs of getting back to work and the fact that you are back at work stronger than ever, you can add to the powerful tribe of visible returner role models.

I hope you'll support future returners in this way. And, perhaps in other ways too: by mentoring someone else returning from a career break or by actively looking to bring returners into your own team, if you reach the point at which you're hiring people yourself.

Finally, how better to end this book than by hearing from successful returners themselves: back at work, stronger than ever, and viewing their break as a hugely valuable part of their lifetime career.

'I am so much better at my job now than I was before my career break. I've got more perspective, I'm more resilient and I don't take myself so seriously.' Mia, now back at work as a regulatory advisor, after a five-year break

'Without my break I would never have had the headspace or courage to change careers. I would still be stressed and unhappy. Now I head off to work so full of energy and ideas.' Jo, now back at work as an AI apprentice, after a two-year break

'I always used to second-guess myself. But I did so many things on my career break that I never imagined I'd be able to do. Now, back at work, I don't hesitate before throwing myself in. I know just how capable I am.' Joao, now back at work as a risk manager, after a seven-year break

'I feel like someone has flipped a switch in my head and I'm back to who I was seven years ago, only more empathetic and definitely more patient.' Mandeep, now back at work as a graphic designer, after a seven-year break

References
(in order of appearance)

Chapter 1

Hanson, Rick, *Hardwiring Happiness: The Practical Science of Reshaping Your Brain and Your Life*, Rider, 2013

Ito, T.A., Larsen, J.T., Smith, N.K. and Cacioppo, J.T. (1998), 'Negative information weighs more heavily on the brain: The Negativity bias in evaluative categorizations', *Journal of Personality and Social Psychology*, 75(4), 887–900

Kahneman, Daniel and Tversky, Amos (1979), 'Prospect theory: An analysis of decision under risk', *Econometrica*, 47, 263–22

Larsen, R.J., and Prizmic, Z. (2009), 'Regulation of emotional well-being: Overcoming the hedonic treadmill', in S.J. Lopez and C.R. Snyder (eds), *The Oxford Handbook of Positive Psychology* (2nd ed., pp. 258–68), Oxford University Press

Darwin, Charles, *The Expression of the Emotions in Man and Animals*, London, John Murray, 1872

Frank, Robert H., *Passions within Reason: The Strategic Role of the Emotions*, New York, Norton, 1988

Greenhaus, J. H., and Beutell, N. J. (1985), 'Sources and conflict between work and family roles', *Academy of Management Review*, 10(1), 76–88

Greenhaus, J.H., and Powell, G.N. (2006), 'When work and family are allies: A theory of work-family enrichment', *Academy of Management Review*, 31(1), 72–92

Aryee, S., Srinivas, E.S., and Tan, H.H. (2005), 'Rhythms of life: Antecedents and outcomes of work-family balance in employed parents', *Journal of Applied Psychology*, 90(1), 132–46

Curran, Thomas, *The Perfection Trap*, London, Cornerstone Press, 2023 (p. 17)

Hewitt., P.L. and Flett, G.L. (1991), 'Perfectionism in the self and social contexts: Conceptualisation, assessment and association with psychopathology', *Journal of Personality and Social Psychology*, 60(3), 456–70

Curran, T. and Hill, A.P. (2019), 'Perfectionism is increasing over time: A meta-analysis of birth cohort differences from 1989 to 2016', *Psychological Bulletin*, 145(4), 410–29

Harari, D., Swider, B.W., Steed, L.B. and Breidenthal, A.P. (2018), 'Is perfect good? A meta-analysis of perfectionism in the workplace', *Journal of Applied Psychology*, 103(10), 1121–44

Hill, A.P., Hall, H.K. and Appleton, P.R. (2011), 'The cognitive, affective and behavioural responses of self-oriented perfectionists following successive failure on a muscular endurance test', *International Journal of Sport and Exercise Psychology*, 9, 189–207

Kanter, Rosabeth Moss, 'The imperfect balance between work and life', *Harvard Business Review*, 28 August 2012

Bridges, William, *Transitions: Making Sense of Life's Changes*, Boston, Da Capo Press, 2004

Chapter 2

Robertson, Ian, *How Confidence Works: The New Science of Self-Belief*, London, Transworld, 2021

Hügelschäfer, S. and Achtziger, A. (2014), 'On confident men and rational women: It's all on your mid(set)', *Journal of Economic Psychology*, 41, 31–44

Govindji, R. and Linley, P.A. (2007), 'Strengths use, self-concordance and well-being: Implications for strengths coaching and coaching psychologists', *International Coaching Psychology Review*, 2(2), 143–53

Proctor, C., Maltby, J. and Linley, P.A. (2009), 'Strengths use as a predictor of well-being and health-related quality of life', *Journal of Happiness Studies*, 10, 583–630

Roth, T., *Strengthsfinder 2.0*, New York, Gallup Press, 2007

Wood, A.M., Linley, P.A., Maltby, J. and Kashdan, T.B. (2010), 'Using personal and psychological strengths leads to increases in wellbeing over time: A longitudinal study and the development of the Strengths Use Questionnaire', *Personality and Individual Differences*, 50(1)

Linley, P.A., Nielsen, K.M., Wood, A.M., Gillett, R. and Biswas-Diener, R. (2010), 'Using signature strengths in pursuit of goals: Effects on goal progress, need satisfaction, and well-being, and implications for coaching psychologists', *International Coaching Psychology Review*, 5(1), 8–17

Harter, J.K., Schmidt, F.L., and Hayes, T.L. (2002), 'Business-unit-level relationship between employee satisfaction, employee engagement, and business outcomes: A meta-analysis', *Journal of Applied Psychology*, 87, 268–79

Yeager, D.S., Hanselman, P., Walton, G.M., Murray, J.S., Crosnoe, R., Muller, C., Dweck, C.S, et al. (2019), 'A national experiment reveals where a growth mindset improves achievement', *Nature*, 573, 364–9

Pauwels, L., Chalavi, S. and Swinnen, S.P. (2018), 'Aging and brain plasticity', *Aging*, 10(8), 1789–90

Rossi, E., Cheng, H., Kroll, J.F., Diaz, M.T. and Newman, S.D. (2017), 'Changes in white-matter connectivity in late second language learners: Evidence from diffusion tensor imaging', *Frontiers in Psychology*, 8

Dweck, Carol, *Mindset: Changing the Way You Think to Fulfil Your Potential* (6th ed.), London, Robinson, 2017

Chapter 3

Bandura, Albert, *Self-Efficacy: The Exercise of Control*, New York, W.H. Freeman and Company, 1997

Gartzia, L., Morgenroth, T., Ryan, M.K. and Peters, K. (2021), 'Testing the motivational effects of attainable role models: Field and experimental evidence', *Journal of Theoretical Social Psychology*, 5(4), 591–602

Chapter 4

Seligman, M.E.P., *Flourish: A Visionary New Understanding of Happiness and Well-Being*, New York, Free Press, 2011

Kim, A. and Maglio, S.J. (2018), 'Vanishing time in the pursuit of happiness', *Psychonomic Bulletin & Review*, 25, 1337–42

Mauss, I.B., Tamir, M., Anderson, C.L., and Savino, N.S. (2011), 'Can seeking happiness make people unhappy? Paradoxical effects of valuing happiness', *Emotion*, 11(4), 807–15

Chapter 5

O'Keefe, P.A., Dweck, C.S. and Walton, G.M. (2018), 'Implicit theories of interest: Finding your passion or developing it?', *Psychological Science,* 29(10), 1653–64

Schwartz, Barry, *The Paradox of Choice: Why More is Less*, London, HarperCollins, 2004

Iyengar, S.S. and Lepper, M.R. (2000), 'When choice is demotivating: Can one desire too much of a good thing?', *Journal of Personality and Social Psychology*, 79(6), 995–1006

Ibarra, Herminia, *Working Identity: Unconventional Strategies for Reinventing Your Career* (2nd ed.), Cambridge, MA, Harvard Business Review Press, 2023

Kahneman, D., *Thinking Fast and Slow*, London, Penguin, 2012

Dijksterhuis, A. (2004), 'Think different: The merits of unconscious thought in preference development and decision making', *Journal of Personality and Social Psychology*, 87(5), 586–98

Dijksterhuis, A. and Nordgren, L.F. (2006), 'A theory of unconscious thought', *Perspectives on Psychological Science*, 1(2), 95–109

Creswell J.D., Bursley J.K. and Satpute, A.B. (2013), 'Neural reactivation links unconscious thought to decision-making performance', *Social Cognitive and Affective Neuroscience*, 8(8), 863–9

Chapter 6

Asch, S.E. (1946), 'Forming impressions of personality', *Journal of Abnormal and Social Psychology*, 41(3), 258–90

Glanzer, M. and Cunitz, A.R. (1966), 'Two storage mechanisms in free recall', *Journal of Verbal Learning and Verbal Behavior*, 5(4), 351–60

Booker, C., *The Seven Basic Plots: Why We Tell Stories*, London, Continuum, 2005

Storr, Will, *The Science of Storytelling: Why Stories Make Us Human and How To Tell Them Better*, London, William Collins, 2019

Thorndike, E.L. (1920), 'A constant error in psychological ratings', *Journal of Applied Psychology*, 4(1), 25–9

Chapter 7

Fuller, J., Raman, M., Sage-Gavin, E., Hines, K. et al., *Hidden Workers: Untapped Talent*, Cambridge, MA, Harvard Business School Project on Managing the Future of Work and Accenture, 2023

Weisshaar, K. (2021), 'Employment lapses and subsequent hiring disadvantages: An experimental approach examining types of discrimination and mechanisms', *Socius*, 7

Lössbroek, Jelle, Lancee, Bram, van der Lippe, Tanja and Schippers, Joop (2021), 'Age discrimination in hiring decisions: A factorial survey among managers in nine European countries', *European Sociological Review*, 37(1), 49–66

Wiseman, Richard, *The Luck Factor: The Scientific Study of the Lucky Mind*, London, Arrow, 2004

Schneider, S. L. (2001), 'In search of realistic optimism: Meaning, knowledge, and warm fuzziness', *American Psychologist*, 56(3), 250–63

Seligman, M.E. (1998; 2006), *Learned Optimism: How to Change Your Mind and Your Life*, New York, Vintage

Chapter 9

Mair, Carolyn, *The Psychology of Fashion (The Psychology of Everything)*, Abingdon, Routledge, 2018

Adam, H. and Galinsky, A.D. (2012), 'Enclothed cognition', *Journal of Experimental Social Psychology*, 48(4), 918–25

Bridges, William, *Transitions: Making Sense of Life's Changes*, Boston, Da Capo Press, 2004

Chapter 10

Clance, P.R., and Imes, S.A. (1978), 'The imposter phenomenon in high achieving women: Dynamics and therapeutic intervention', *Psychotherapy: Theory, Research & Practice*, 15(3), 241–7

Bravata, D.M., Watts, S.A., Keefer, A.L., Madhusudhan, D.K., Taylor, K.T., Clark, D.M., Nelson, R.S., Cokley, K.O. and Hagg, H.K. (2020), 'Prevalence, predictors, and treatment of impostor syndrome: A systematic review', *Journal of General Internal Medicine*, 35(4), 1252–75

Kossek, E.E., Lautsch, B.A. and Eaton, S.C. (2006), 'Telecommuting, control, and boundary management: Correlates of policy use and practice, job control, and work-family effectiveness', *Journal of Vocational Behavior*, 68, 347–67

Kossek, E. E. and Lautsch, B., *CEO of Me: Creating a Life that Works in the Flexible Job Age*, London and Upper Saddle River, NJ, Financial Times/Pearson Prentice Hall, 2007

Desrochers, S. and Morgan, C. (2021), 'Boundary theory and work-family border theory research: A focus on boundary enactment', *Work and Family Encyclopedia*

Acknowledgements

I've been thinking about writing this book for the past fifteen years – ever since I ran my first return-to-work coaching workshops around my kitchen table. Writing *Return Journey* has truly been a journey in itself! Over the years, many wonderful people have contributed to expanding my knowledge and experience, while others have been an essential part of my practical and emotional support team. You have all ultimately enabled me to create the book I wish I'd had by my side when I was returning to work after my own career break.

At the outset, special thanks go to Katerina, my co-founder in 2012 of Back to Your Future, a back-to-work blog, and in 2014 of Women Returners (now Career Returners), an organisation on a mission to make career breaks a normal part of a lifetime career. Your partnership laid the foundation for everything that followed.

Throughout the journey, I owe deep gratitude to all the brilliant past and present members of the Women/Career Returners team. In particular, to Hazel, for standing shoulder-to-shoulder with me as we built the organisation over the last decade – and for giving me a much-needed nudge to stop talking about writing a book and start doing it! And to Karen, whose expertise has elevated our Career Returners coaching into world-leading programmes, the content of which forms an integral component of the book.

In shaping each chapter, I'm thankful to all the returners whose stories inspired the case studies – your experiences, learnings and wisdom were invaluable in bringing the psychology and coaching exercises to life. I'm so proud of all the members of our returner community who have found their path back to fulfilling work with such courage and persistence. Thanks also to our pioneering Career Returners employers, for partnering with us to develop and refine the supportive returner programmes and pathways that significantly informed the final section.

In bringing this book to life, I'm grateful to my lifelong friend Jane, for sharing your own writing experience and for your encouragement that I was also up to the task. To my agent Victoria, for your belief that this was a book worth writing. To Pippa, for your support and insight through the writing process. And to Elena and the Piatkus team, thank you for so skilfully guiding this debut author from draft copy to a polished finished product.

Finally, my warmest thanks to my amazing family. To Dominic, for your unwavering love and support throughout both my own winding return-to-work journey, and the ups and downs of our work–life rollercoaster ever since. To Isobel and Oliver, you are my touchstones and my most cherished cheerleaders. And to my mother, Audrey, thank you for building my self-belief and for showing me that it's never too late to embrace new challenges.